BEING THE
MOM

BEING THE
MOM

EMILY WATTS

BOOKCRAFT

Salt Lake City, Utah

Bookcraft is a registered trademark of Deseret Book Company.

Visit us at www.deseretbook.com

Library of Congress Cataloging-in-Publication Data

Watts, Emily.
  Being the mom : 10 coping strategies I learned by accident because I had children on purpose / Emily Watts.
     p.   cm.
  ISBN 1-57008-825-X (pbk.)
  1. Motherhood. 2. Child rearing. 3. Life skills. I. Title.
  HQ759 .W355 2002
  649'.1--dc21   2002001077

Printed in the United States of America   72076
Publishers Printing, Salt Lake City, UT

10   9   8   7   6

To my gems:
Natalie, Brandon, Trevor,
Dylan, and Sylvia

And to Larry,
the jewel who is their father

Contents

Being the Mom

I distinctly remember every detail of the beautiful April morning when they wheeled me out of my hospital room down to the curbside with my brand-new baby daughter and deposited us in the waiting car. My husband was beaming, my baby was sleeping, and I was nodding and smiling behind vases of pink carnations and rosebuds, trying not to cry or show the panic I felt. They were sending me out into the world to do this all by myself! There was no nurse waiting a button away to rush in and say, "Shall I take her back to the nursery for you now so you can get some rest?" No one would be handing me a menu each day with choices for three meals plus an evening snack. No one would be there to wave a vial of smelling salts under my nose if I felt faint in the shower, or to stand at my elbow to be sure I was supporting the baby's head properly when I held her.

I was on my own. I was the Mom now.

I thought I had some notion of what being the Mom would entail. My own mother had set a great example for me. I had in fact apprenticed for years, often tending my younger brothers and baby-sitting on a regular basis as a teenager. My husband and I had filled in several times to care for our friends' kids, sometimes for a whole weekend!

It turns out that such experiences don't prepare you to be the Mom any better than substituting a few times for the CTR 5s in Primary would prepare you to be a full-time kindergarten teacher. Interacting with children is a world away from having ultimate responsibility for them. As I laid that little girl in her cradle, the truth washed over me again that this was a lifetime commitment we had made. We had made it joyfully, willingly, even longingly, but that didn't mean we really knew what we were getting in for.

I have sometimes wondered if that pre-parental view of parenthood isn't a little like the premortal view we might have had of mortality. We saw the plan of salvation, we recognized the possibilities, and we joined in shouting for joy. Then we got down here to earth and actually started living it. I'll admit that there have been plenty of times when I've wondered, Was I so busy shouting for joy that I missed this part in the premortal lecture? Did I really sign up for this on purpose? What was I *thinking?*

Being the Mom carries some of those same feelings. I knew in a theoretical sense, for example, that I would probably be helping kids with homework, but somehow that didn't translate in my brain to the numbing reality of staying up past midnight hot-gluing pieces of macaroni to a half-sphere of Styrofoam to make a model of the mitochondria in a cell. I knew that peanut butter would figure largely in my life with children, but I didn't anticipate having to make the exact same sandwich, cut in precisely the same four triangles with the crusts off, 9,125 times. (Not to mention being forced to eat 9,125 bread crusts because it seemed wasteful to throw them away.) I didn't realize either that every time I nudged a child up to the front of the chapel on Mother's Day, I would feel the same swelling in my heart, a fierce, almost uncontainable surge of love connecting that child to me in a tangible, eternal bond.

I guess what I'm trying to say is that I always knew being the Mom would be wonderful, and I knew it would be hard. I just didn't know how wonderful—or how hard—until I got in and started doing it. So my strategies for coping with the challenges and capturing the joy developed quite by accident over the years as I sorted out what worked for our family and what didn't.

I have now been the Mom for more than twenty-one years. I have taken that wheelchair ride from the maternity ward to the curb five times—six, counting the little one we didn't get to keep—and recently we took that first baby daughter and her little brother and dropped them both off at a curbside of their own: the one at the Missionary Training Center. I have loved being the Mom—and, at moments, I have hated it. I have laughed myself silly and cried myself to sleep, burst with pride and withered with embarrassment, felt so much love for my children I thought I might float away and been so frustrated with them I feared I might wrench their little heads clean off their little necks.

What interests me most about being the Mom, though, is how it reveals me to myself. Years of sorting through life with never enough time, enough energy, or enough money to do everything that seemed important have taught me what really *is* important to me. Having my behavior, my words, and even my attitude reflected back to me through the innocent lens of my children's actions has helped me reconsider my ways often and try harder to be good. Sharing the same space with a small flock of other free agents has taught me a lot about getting along, getting by, and getting on with things.

I don't pretend to have acquired any vast wisdom, but I *have* managed to pick up an idea or two along the way, usually after being repeatedly smacked in the face with it. I know there have been lots of times in my life when I have felt guilty, inadequate, or just plain stupid, and I've always felt better when my friends have admitted that they have felt that way too. The "coping strategies" I've presented in this book are really just hints to help nudge you past some of those rough spots in the road. They're the verbal equivalent of friends going to lunch together, an attempt to sort things out and share and laugh and go back home ready to try again.

Ultimately, that's what being the Mom seems to be mostly about: trying again, and again, and again, if need be, until something finally clicks. That may just be the best coping strategy of all.

Instead of Acquiring More Things, Use the Things You Have More Creatively

In the ward where I have lived practically my entire married life, my inadequacy at anything that requires manual dexterity is well-nigh legendary. This includes knitting, crocheting, applying paint to small blocks of wood, gluing anything with a hot-glue gun, and sewing. Particularly sewing, which of course involves not just the combined hand-and-foot skill required to run a piece of light machinery but also cutting with scissors and putting things together in a logical fashion. The governing principle of my life as a seamstress seems to be: If any two pieces of material can be joined incorrectly, that's the way I will sew them together.

So I don't do much sewing—an accommodation that results in less fraying of fabric and of nerves in my life. But when my children were small I did sew two things that served us well for many years: a red cape and a black cape. They were what we used for Halloween costumes in a year when we were squeezing every dollar pretty tightly. One child wanted to be a bat (not Batman, mind you), and another wanted to be Superman. The fabric was cheap but durable, and I didn't use a pattern, just gathered up one end of a rectangle of cloth and stitched a "waistband" to it with the ends sticking out several inches so they could be tied together.

As it turned out, the black cape outlasted the stage of my son's life where he basically lived as a bat, rolling himself up in it for quiet indoor pursuits and flapping it in the breeze when he played outside. It later became a Dracula cape, a zombie cape, a witch's cape, and a cape for The Shadow. I think it may even have shown up one year on the Ghost of Christmas Yet to Come in our annual Noel nod to Charles Dickens. The red cape, in its turn, adorned Little Red Riding Hood, a devil, a prince, and Snow White, to name a few. Those capes were a staple of our dress-up box for many years.

That was the seed of my understanding the principle that things you can use in lots of ways are almost always better, cheaper, or more fun than things that have only one specific use. This is true of toys, kitchen utensils, clothing, and a host of other stuff.

For example, we bought a new dishwasher when our oldest child was six, and the large box in which it was delivered became immediately the best toy we had ever bought. It was a playhouse, a clubhouse, and later, with a window cut in one side, a grocery store and a puppet theater. Furnished with a pillow and stuffed animal, it frequently served as a quiet sanctuary—big enough for three children but zero adults. We kept that box for months, maybe even years, and when it finally fell apart and we threw it away, our daughter reprimanded us for not doing it at night when she wouldn't see.

Contrast that with the expensive mechanical dog that we suckered for, partly out of guilt because I couldn't handle the thought of a real dog at that point in my mothering career. It was quite a wonder when it worked properly, which it did fully a third of the time. It would come when you called it, lurching forward on unbending motorized legs until it tipped onto its side to lie helplessly waving those legs in the air. The kids had fun for about a week putting that dog through its paces.

The problem was, that was all the dog was good for. Its mechanisms made it heavy and awkward to carry around;

it wasn't cuddly and comforting like the stuffed tiger our little boy took to bed with him every night for four years. Because it came with its own tricks, the children didn't invest any of *their* imagination in it, and so it never became precious to them. But we had paid a lot for it, so I couldn't just give it away. It took up space and added to the clutter of our house for years, reminding my subconscious mind every time I stumbled across it that I had made a poor buying decision and, worse, that I had made it out of guilt because I was too weak, too selfish, to let my children have a real dog. (If there is guilt to be suffered anywhere in the vicinity, I will sniff it out and make it my own.)

I have learned since the dog debacle that our possessions own us almost as fully as we own them. Everything we bring into our homes and lives requires a little piece of our time and attention to care for it: to keep it clean, to store it or display it, to maintain its functionality. So I think we need to be selective and choose to hang on to things that "give back" in an emotional sense as much as they extract.

This, of course, will vary quite a lot based on the size of one's house and one's family and one's income, although it does seem true that in any home, possessions will swell to fill the space allotted to them. It's just a matter of deciding what *kinds* of things will occupy that space. My aunt, for example, has an entire closet full of shoes. She loves shoes, and she can usually be found wearing a pair that perfectly matches her outfit, even if that outfit is a brightly colored plaid. (I'm not exaggerating; my aunt really does have a pair of bright plaid shoes.) This is not a matter of vanity—it's almost more of a hobby, something that she enjoys and can afford and has room for. My own feet are too large and my house too small to accommodate that much footwear, so I don't have it. Anyway, if I wore a pair of bright plaid shoes, I'd look like an advance guard for the Ringling Brothers.

I have another friend who has a room full of fabric— shelves and shelves, stacked with material of all kinds, as well as sophisticated cutting and measuring devices whose uses are as foreign to me as the applications of advanced calculus. When her daughter needed a prom dress, she didn't go from store to store wringing her hands at the scarcity of sleeves and the lowness of necklines and the steepness of prices. A skilled seamstress, she simply had her daughter leaf through some magazines and point out what she liked, and then she sewed it up.

In my friend's life, her stacks of fabric are a symbol of

her skill and her interests, readily available for her to put to a variety of creative uses. Transferred to my life, they would become an indictment of my homemaking clumsiness, a pile of clutter, evidence of my unfulfilled good intentions.

Occasionally someone in my family has a specific sewing need, usually for a school class, for which I have to buy fabric. I used to save the remnants from those projects because I believed somewhere in my heart that a good, frugal, creative woman would find a way to use those bits of cloth, as I know my sewing friend would have. Now I throw them away as soon as the project is complete, and I never have to think about them again.

My own particular weakness in the arena of possessions is books. I have more books than I can ever imagine reading again in this lifetime, although I have read most of them at least once. I just love to be surrounded by books. I love how they look, I love to take one off the shelf and read just a bit from it that I know will uplift and encourage me, and I love to stumble across a new idea or a fresh way of articulating an old idea. Books are an expression of my interest as well as my vocation, so I have devoted a larger proportion of my own space to them than have most of my friends. This may seem frivolous or fruitless or at least unnecessarily dusty to some, but it fills a larger emotional need for me.

So, in order to indulge myself in collecting what I love, I've learned to double up in other areas. I have one rectangular glass baking dish that I use virtually every time I make a cake, a casserole, or a Jell-O salad. (If I have to do two of those items for the same meal, though, I'm in trouble.) My cookie sheets are large jelly-roll pans that do extra duty as breakfast-in-bed trays and Play-Doh/puzzle holders for sick children, and they're just the right size to accommodate our family's favorite brand of frozen pizza. I have abandoned the various lap desks and clipboards and other portable flat surfaces I used to buy for my children, who have a thing against doing homework sitting up to a table. Those items never got any use because the kids would always just pull a book from the bookcase to serve as a lap table when they sat down to work. I can say honestly that when our older children were in elementary school we used our children's encyclopedias every day—not, perhaps, in the way their authors envisioned, but we certainly did use them.

I like to apply the same principle in the way I grocery shop and cook. If I have several different recipes for ground beef, for example, I don't necessarily have to tie myself down to one specific meal on a given night. About half the time when I try to plan a week's worth of menus, I don't feel like fixing or eating what I planned for by the time its day comes around. If I can at least choose on the spur of the moment between spaghetti and tacos and meat loaf and tater tot casserole, I have a better chance of actually being motivated to cook dinner that evening.

As far as meal preparation goes, on any given night, I generally end up throwing either time or money at it. They're almost interchangeable where food is concerned. There are so many amazing things you can buy that cook up in just a few minutes—but they tend to cost way more than food cooked from scratch does. So, because of the guilt factor, I never used to buy them.

Then I figured out how much money we were actually spending to eat out on those nights when I just couldn't face the thought of making dinner, or when I got hung up at work and didn't get home in time to make what I'd planned. Suddenly the quick-to-fix meals began to look like a real bargain by comparison. Now I try to always have two or three of those things—a frozen lasagna, meat pies, an all-in-one skillet dinner—on hand as backup, and it's almost a game to see how long I can go without having to use them. Regardless of how my day goes, I can relax in at least one area of life because I know my family will get fed.

A nice side benefit of keeping open a variety of options is that it shakes you loose of the notion that there's One Right Way to do something. You develop the habit of noticing many acceptable means to an end. And doesn't it make sense that having an increased number of options for achieving a goal would dramatically improve your chances of lighting on something that works?

My parents live across town from us, and as our children get old enough to drive, it is always a source of anxiety to them to make their first solo trip to their grandparents' house. As we're giving them directions, we don't take them along the familiar route we've traveled for years—it's a little too complicated to explain, and there's a lot of shifting around on the freeway, which is scary when you're sixteen. We tell them instead to get on State Street, turn left, drive and drive and drive until they come to 800 South, turn right, and drive some more until they get up into Emigration Canyon, and they can find the house easily at that point. If they get lost or confused, we tell them, they can take just about any north-south road and it will get them to 800 South eventually, and then it's a straight shot from there up the canyon. They don't usually lose their way, and it calms them down just to know that there are many alternatives that will bring them to the desired destination.

Just as there are many "right" ways to get to my parents' house, there are many "right" ways to accomplish most tasks in life. Take preparing a Relief Society lesson, for example. I've seen teachers who were masters at the object lesson; others who always had a handout; some who were strong on visual aids or other enhancements, such as special musical numbers; some who always typed out quotes for class members to read; and some who were great at getting a good discussion going. They were all wonderful teachers, but each had her own distinctive style. I hope none of them ever thought they were doing it "wrong" because their methods differed from someone else's. And I particularly hope that no one ever felt obligated to pass out handouts that she didn't have the time or the inclination to make in the first place!

If you have the guiding principle foremost in your mind, it's easier to relax about how you're going to get there. My teenage drivers knew they needed to get to 800 South somehow. I know, when I'm teaching Relief Society, that I want the sisters to feel the Spirit, to be uplifted, and to be helped in a practical way—but there are lots of ways to make that happen! If my goal is a clean house, I try not to obsess about who does which chores in what order. I find that I stay a lot calmer and better able to cope when I can find the techniques and tools that maximize my skills and satisfy my passions.

Really, these are two sides of the same coin: try increasing your options and decreasing your possessions, and see how much easier life can become!

Learn to Laugh: Today's Embarrassment Will Likely Be Tomorrow's Comedy

When I was a teenager, I had a recurring fantasy that someday I might be thought of as graceful. I was tall—"five-foot-twelve" I sometimes told people in an effort to avoid acknowledging my full six feet—and had long since abandoned any hope of being petite or cute. But "graceful" didn't seem so unreasonable a trait to imagine possessing: supermodels were tall and graceful, after all, and ballerinas, and basketball players.

However, I was not inherently graceful. In fact, in a letter I found recently in my parents' attic, my father described me as being, at age four, "bright and well coordinated rhythmically but not physically dexterous." Apparently I had a habit even then of marring my doll-like countenance in a series of close encounters with the sidewalk and other uneven surfaces.

My fondest daydream was of myself running down the slight incline at the end of our high school football field, my long hair flowing out behind me, and a handsome boy of at least seventeen watching from across the field and thinking, "Who is that girl? I wonder if she's been asked to Homecoming yet?" In reality, whenever I did anything like attempt to run in the vicinity of even a mildly good-looking boy between the ages of twelve and eighteen, my legs had a vicious tendency to get all tangled up. I learned later to recognize this as the fight-or-flight syndrome—all the blood leaving my peripheral limbs to keep my heart pumping and my brain alive—but being able to put a scientific tag on it was cold comfort.

As a young adult, I was once sitting in a stake conference session, checking my watch regularly because I had to slip out early. I was purposely sitting on the front row of the overflow area so I wouldn't have to climb out over anyone's legs, but the only entrance open was on the other side of the chapel. My intention was to make my exit as swiftly and silently as possible.

When the moment arrived, I stood and quickly moved toward the door. I stumbled a little on my left leg as I took my first step, but even that was not enough to signal me that said leg was completely asleep and would not support my body. No, I found that out with the next step I tried to take, when I shifted my full weight to that useless appendage and went down like a bag of wet cement.

I heard the collective gasp of the several dozen people who saw me fall, and I lay still for a moment, assessing what had happened and whether I was injured and what my best option would be. Then I started to giggle, unleashing a murmur of palpable relief among the spectators and prompting my good friend Larry, who later became my good husband, to hurry over and help hustle me out of there.

This was by no means an unusual incident in my life. Another time, I was trying to leave treats anonymously on the doorstep of some fellows in our Young Adult group. I rang the doorbell and began to dash away, neglecting to notice that they had one of those little wire fences resembling a series of croquet hoops lining their walk. The inevitability that my foot would catch one of those loops was as good as predestined. I was sprawled on the ground, helpless with laughter, when the guys came to the door to retrieve the treats.

Then there was the time my husband and I went to a

21

February basketball game at the University of Utah. The snow was piled high that winter, and he dropped me, his seven-months-pregnant wife, off at the arena because it was clear he was going to have to park the car out in the north forty somewhere. After the game, he ran out ahead to bring the car around to the entrance to the parking lot so I wouldn't have to scale any of the snowdrifts along the way. This seemed like a good plan, but it did leave me to negotiate a short stretch of slippery pavement unassisted. When I went down that time, I was pretty much a beached whale, forced by ice and my own girth to lie there until help arrived. Fortunately, my husband's head popped up over a snowdrift shortly thereafter; having seen my own head bob along and then suddenly disappear, he didn't take long to discern what had happened. In fact, after two decades of marriage he now reaches for my arm instinctively whenever we approach a potentially hazardous irregularity in the sidewalk, because he knows it's easier to hold me up than to scrape me up.

This all just goes to show that I've had plenty of opportunities to learn that although something may seem terribly embarrassing at the moment it happens, unless you have actually suffered bodily harm, you'll probably be laughing about it later. And this can be true for more than just physical gaffes, if you choose to let it. I don't fall so often anymore—I'm usually just not moving fast enough to put myself in peril—but I still get embarrassed, and I'm still learning to laugh about it.

Sometimes the effort you make to avoid embarrassment just gets you in deeper. I'm remembering an occasion quite early in our marriage when we traveled to Europe with my parents and all my siblings. The hotel accommodations in France were such that we had to double up one night, and my twenty-one-year-old brother stayed in the room with my husband and me. The next morning, I took advantage of his slipping out for breakfast to jump into the bathtub. When I got out, I discovered that he had returned, and I was trapped in the bathroom without a robe. The towels in that particular hotel had clearly been designed for the petite Frenchwoman rather than the statuesque American-Amazon, and I found that a horizontal draping did not provide sufficient vertical coverage. Ever resourceful, I held the towel vertically to cover the front of me and slid out of the bathroom with my back against the wall so no one could see. I inched carefully along, past a dresser and a closet, while my brother watched me with a strange, amused expression on his face. When I got safely to the bed and grabbed the blanket to wrap up in, I couldn't help crowing, "There! Didn't I handle that well?"

"Yeah," said my brother, "except for that mirror behind you." I had somehow failed to notice that the closet door was a full-length mirror!

Another classic example of the folly of trying consciously to avoid embarrassment was shared with me by my good friend Laurel. She tells of being on a date with a young man she really wanted to impress. She was *so* prepared for this elegant evening; in fact, the Relief Society in her university ward had recently devoted a homemaking night to practicing the finer points of dining etiquette. So when she found herself at dinner with a bite containing one of those unmanageable bits of gristle that seem to plague even the most immaculately prepared chicken, she knew exactly what to do. One delicately lifts a utensil to the mouth, removes the offending morsel, and places it discreetly on the side of one's plate.

If she hadn't had the etiquette lesson, she probably would have done what most of us would do: spit the piece into her napkin and have done with it. But no, thank goodness she had been saved from that faux pas. Carefully, she moved the fork to her mouth. Delicately, she extracted the glob of unchewable meat. As fate would have it, however, the piece of chicken flipped off the fork en route to the plate. And it didn't just fall into her lap, which would have been embarrassing enough. It took a bad bounce off the table and landed squarely in the middle of her date's plate! He had his head turned and didn't notice what had happened, but when she looked up she saw that the other couple who were with them had seen the whole thing.

All right, Miss Manners. What does one do now?

Nothing, apparently. Just die a thousand deaths, try not to choke when the man of your dreams turns back to his dinner, and live in agony as you imagine the conversation those two men will have after they have dropped off their dates. My friend said she was sure her life was over that night, but of course now, years later, it's just another story in the archives of nightmare-date annals to which we all could contribute.

It's pretty funny when we dig our own graves that way, but it can be a little harder to laugh at embarrassments that come unbidden from outside sources. I have learned from years of practice, though, how important it can be to find the humor in such incidents, difficult as that may seem. In this regard, my sorest and silliest trials are often related to the shape of my body. (I *am* in shape. Round is a shape.) I was a thin woman once. But when I had children, I put on weight, and even though it never seemed like much weight at the time, when you multiply it by five children, it amounts to . . . well, rather a lot. Add to that the fact that it was pregnancy weight I was retaining, and that I basically gave up on trying to regain any semblance of my original abdominal musculature after child number three, and you will have the framework for what follows.

I offer one example, representative of many. I was in the temple, wearing my circa-1982 polyester/ironweave temple dress, and one of the sweet matrons patted my hand as I was heading for the escalator and said, "Bless your heart, when is your baby due?"

Now, on that particular day I was not pregnant. I had not been pregnant for more than eight years, and had no plans to be pregnant ever again in this life. But I was wearing a dress that I had bought when I *was* pregnant on a fairly regular basis, and since I tend to carry my extra weight right out in front and still have the slender wrists and ankles I had when I was a thin woman, I could see that it was an honest mistake—and one that she was by no means the first person to make.

Still, I never know quite what to say when this happens to me. Usually I just laugh lightly and say, "Oh, I'm not pregnant (ha-ha)." This is awkward for both me and the offending party, though, because the next line is always a stunned and stuttered apology, "Oh, my gosh, I'm so sorry, I mean . . . I just thought . . ." and then I feel obligated to try to set the person at ease: "It's all right, really, it happens all the time," which is just another way of admitting that *everyone* in the world knows that I weigh too much.

I used to go home and cry, or at least sulk, when this happened to me. But one day I took a good, hard look at the truth, which was that I wasn't planning to do anything about my weight anytime soon because I knew how much emotional energy it would take, and I didn't have that energy to spare right then. Thus it was a logical fallacy to expend even more emotional energy moping about a situation I had already decided to live with. So instead I started composing clever answers in my mind. I have never used any of these, mind you, but it makes me feel better just to have them in my arsenal.

Answer 1:

"When is your baby due?"

"Due to what?"

Answer 2:

"When is your baby due?"

"Six weeks." See, I might look pregnant, but I don't look seven and a half *months* pregnant, so I can say this and then wait for the person to tell me how fabulous I look, which I need right then.

Answer 3 (my personal favorite, given to me by my friend Janette Rallison):

"When is your baby due?"

"I'm not a pregnant woman, but I play one on TV."

The thing I find the most amusing, though, is not that people sometimes mistake me for being pregnant but that people in general are so incredibly proprietary about pregnancy in the first place. It's the only condition I have experienced in which total strangers seem utterly comfortable coming up and patting you on the stomach. I suppose that's rather sweet, really, a sort of vicarious admiring of your baby before he or she is actually available to be admired in person. But it cracks me up.

It's good practice, I guess, for when that baby does come, because having children is a surefire formula for embarrassment. And unpredictability being a key component in both embarrassment and comedy, parenting is a fairly funny occupation all around.

This is largely because the little darlings don't yet have the filter to help them know what's appropriate and tactful to say, so they just say what's on their minds. When I was teaching Primary to a rambunctious group of four-year-olds, for instance, I was desperate to catch their attention one day and started singing a song. The response was unbelievable—textbook, almost. They fell silent one by one until they were all enraptured, listening quietly. I finished the song, there was a moment of perfect silence, and then one little boy said, in a hushed, awe-filled voice, "Teacher, you sing *awful!*" Apparently they were not enraptured—merely stunned. Oh, well. They were quiet for thirty seconds, anyway.

It can be even more embarrassing when the family character is reflected in the words that drop from those angelic lips. Our two-year-old was sitting on her grandmother's lap, carefully perusing all the little pictures that decorate the margins in the classic book *Mike Mulligan and the Steam Shovel,* when she came upon a drawing of a man who was kicking a flat tire on his truck. "Oh, my," said my mother in that wonderfully enthusiastic voice she always uses with her tinier grandchildren. "What do you suppose that man is saying?" Whereupon my baby girl proceeded to repeat what she had heard her father say in a similar situation, which regrettably is not printable in a polite publication. In fairness to her father, I must say that he almost never said that word, but apparently it made quite an impression the one time he called upon it.

The thing is, you can never be prepared for every eventuality. You can warn children against hot stoves and electric outlets, but does it occur to you to forbid them to microwave a flashlight? You teach them to be loving and kind to each other, not realizing that this might translate in a two-year-old's mind to sharing her Doritos with her newborn brother. (We found traces of nacho cheese powder around his mouth, but there was no lasting damage, thank goodness.) It's cute when a toddler is up in the front of the classroom drawing on the bottom two inches of the chalkboard while you're teaching Gospel Doctrine, but somewhat less cute when with an unerring instinct for mischief he loads up the eraser with chalk dust and flings it at a man in a dark suit.

If eternal vigilance is the price of peace for governments, it is doubly so for mothers. One problem is that you can spend so much time watchdogging your children's behavior that you totally neglect to check in on your own status. I remember especially one Sunday when with particular self-satisfaction I had managed to get our entire herd out the door for church on time. It is ridiculously difficult for our family to do this, given that we live right across the street from the meetinghouse. My theory is that because they can all walk to church by themselves, they don't worry about missing their ride, and pretty soon they've stopped worrying about missing the opening song, prayer, announcements, and so on.

But this week was different—this week we were going to be punctual. I was walking down the driveway and had just turned to wave cheerily to our neighbors who were not of our faith, proud of how every child was all shined up and precious and prompt, when I thought I detected a slightly puzzled look on the man's face. As I turned back around, I happened to catch just a hint of an impression of my shadow, enough to verify that I was on my way to church with a headful of instant curlers. I guess that could have been a lot more embarrassing if I had gotten all the way into the chapel!

I don't suppose I'll ever have it all together—and if I did, I wouldn't know where to put it. So now I just store up those little less-than-perfect moments and save them for the day when time will have seasoned them, turning them magically into a source of delight for our whole family. They're a lot less cumbersome that way, and a lot more fun.

Be Discerning:
Sometimes a One-Mile
Effort Is Enough

Sometime in the latter half of the 1980s, the Utah school system imposed a ban on homemade treats in class because of the potential liabilities that might result from uncontrolled cooking environments. Before this blessed ban, moms used to compete rather ferociously to bring the fanciest, cleverest, or yummiest offerings to school on birthdays and holidays.

My oldest daughter was in kindergarten in those pre-ban days, and one time her teacher wanted to do a "Twelve Days of Christmas" event in her class. The idea was that each day one of the moms would bring some kind of treat based thematically on a verse of the song, such as pears for "partridge in a pear tree." I was assigned "twelve drummers drumming."

I racked my brains for a while and finally lit upon the idea of making gingerbread cookie drums. I didn't have a drum-shaped cookie cutter, but it didn't seem like a very complex shape, and I thought I would just make up a cardboard pattern and cut around it. Having settled that in my mind, I set it aside and didn't think about it again until the day before we were to take our treat to class. (This false complacency is why I live most of my life in crisis mode.)

Finally finding myself at the point where the task could be postponed no longer, I whipped up a batch of ginger-bread dough and set it in the fridge to cool while I figured out the drum pattern. This is where the plan began to go awry. Because I have little artistic talent and even less sense of visual proportion, I couldn't get the drum shrunk down properly in my mind, and my template for the cook-ies ended up being roughly the size of a small TV screen. Naturally, one batch of cookie dough was not enough, and I could fit only four cookies on the baking sheet at a time, so I was mixing and cutting and baking those blasted drums well into the night, sobbing as I piped the last of the frosting onto the last cookie in a crisscross pattern in a futile attempt to make it look like a drum rather than a loosely defined brown blob.

Years later, it occurred to me that those kids would have been just as happy and felt just as drumlike with a Ding Dong and a couple of licorice sticks. Such is the wisdom of hindsight.

The point is, there was nobody standing there in that kindergarten class passing out extra Good Mommy points for those who brought in home-baked treats rather than store-bought ones. No one lingered misty-eyed over those cookies to admire them before gobbling them up. These were five-year-old children; it simply didn't register with them. In subsequent years I guiltlessly picked up a bag of miniature Snickers bars and was every bit as popular with the kindergartners as I had been in the year of the drums.

This set me to wondering if there might be other times when my attempts at second-mile efforts were actually thwarting my effectiveness in the first mile. I learned through brave firsthand experience that I didn't get lynched or even mildly rebuffed if I didn't have handouts for my Relief Society lesson. I figured out that I could cheerfully say yes to a compassionate service assignment if I could pick up a cake or a fruit bowl at the grocery store on the way home from work. I discovered that you can pile potato salad from a deli carton into a nice bowl, put olives around the border of it, and sprinkle some paprika on the top, and people will eat it at a potluck dinner as readily as if you had spent half the day boiling and peeling those potatoes yourself.

I once heard a great story that helped me hone in on this principle a little more clearly. A man had gotten a job cleaning all the phone booths along a certain downtown street. They were the fully enclosed kind with the folding glass doors, and, determined to do a great job, he attacked the first one with vigor, spraying and shining and wiping and polishing until every panel of glass was gleaming, including the top. It took him about two hours. As he stepped back from the booth to admire his work, a mother and her two toddlers crowded into it. The children occupied themselves with smearing chocolatey handprints all over the inside of the glass while their mother talked on the phone. Then a pigeon happened by and left a chalky streak down the outside. It didn't take this man long to figure out that, in his line of work, small, consistent efforts would probably be more effective than large, heroic ones.

If this notion makes you uncomfortable, you may want to collect a few first-mile stratagems that *feel* like second-mile efforts. It was a happy day in my life when I came upon the recipe for "Easy Chicken Bake" in *Lion House Recipes*. Of course, I don't call it that when I make it for my family or for company; I call it "Lion House Chicken," which invests it with a certain authority and makes it sound much fancier than it is. I also adapt the recipe at will to the circumstances in which I am serving it. Here is a loose interpretation:

Ingredients:

However many boneless, skinless chicken breast pieces you need to feed whoever's coming. You can leave the halves whole (that sounds weird, I know, but you get what I mean, don't you?) or cut them into smaller pieces or buy chicken tenders if they're cheaper

Garlic powder

Paprika

Seasoning salt

1 or 2 cans cream of mushroom soup

Milk

Instructions:

Put the chicken in a baking dish large enough to place the pieces flat in one layer. (I usually use my one all-purpose, 13-by-9-inch glass dish.) Sprinkle each piece quite generously with garlic powder, paprika, and seasoning salt. Mix one can cream of mushroom soup with about half a can of milk and pour it over the top. If you're making a bigger batch, use two cans of soup and a whole can of milk. Bake, uncovered, at 350 degrees F. for about an hour.

This takes about five minutes to assemble, and then you can throw it in the oven and ignore it until dinner time. It is very forgiving if you need to leave it in for a few minutes extra or take it out a little earlier. It even makes its own "gravy" with the soup/sauce, which is delicious spooned over mashed potatoes. This is our standard missionaries-over-for-dinner entrée, and because I know how easily it can be done, I'm not nearly as hesitant as I used to be to invite the missionaries to eat with us.

Without meaning to turn this into a cookbook, I find I can't resist sharing one more little dinner trick I was taught by a friend. Put a package of country-style spare ribs in a Crockpot. (All right, take them out of the package first. Let's be accurate here.) Pour a bottle of your favorite barbecue sauce over them and let them simmer on low all day. That's all there is to that one. You can throw in a couple of handfuls of baby carrots if you want, or you can let the kids eat those raw, which they'd probably rather do anyway.

The real virtue in gathering these sorts of ideas is that sometimes we miss out on opportunities to connect with each other because we don't have time or money to do something "special," so we're not comfortable doing anything at all. We lose track of the fact that it's the people who are important, not the menu.

Once when my husband and I were visiting some friends, their teenage son happened to mention that he had never, ever gotten to eat as much pizza as he really wanted. So I invited their family over to dinner at our house with the promise that there would be enough pizza to satisfy everyone. Then I went to the grocery store and picked up seven or eight inexpensive cheese pizzas from their deli, plus an extra block of mozzarella cheese and an assortment of other toppings. Our friends came, we watched a football game on TV and shoveled pizzas in and out of the oven most of the evening, and we had a great time. And, for once in his life, that kid got as much pizza as he could eat.

That was one party that never would have happened if I had been squeamish about serving prefab pizza. We couldn't have afforded seven restaurant pizzas, and I would have been trapped in the kitchen rolling out pizza dough all night if I'd gone the homemade route. The pizza wasn't the important thing—it was just the excuse for getting our families together. In this case, it was better to share the fun and friendship of that first mile than to not stir from home because the second mile would have been unattainable.

Another blessing of knowing when to stop at the first mile is that it leaves you more time and energy to choose to go the second mile on those few occasions when it really does make a difference to do so. Such an occasion arose recently for me when my teenage son asked if he could have a few friends over for a little party. Our home, being small and filled with younger siblings, has not typically been the high-school hangout for our older children, so I was sort of pathetically eager to give this a chance. The dialogue went something like this:

Son: "Can we start at 5:30?"

Mom: "Certainly. Sure. Whatever you want . . . oh. I guess that means you'll want something dinnerlike to eat, right?"

Son: "Uh, yeah, is that okay?"

Mom: "Absolutely. Pizza?"

Son: "Well, the thing is, Ann just had her wisdom teeth out."

Mom, silently to self: *There are girls coming to this party?*

Son: "So is there maybe something softer to eat that would work?"

Mom: "How about chicken noodle soup?"

Son, hopefully: "Homemade?"

Mom: "Of course."

Son: "Really? Wow, that would be great, Mom!"

Now, obviously, homemade chicken noodle soup takes a lot more effort to prepare than frozen pizza. But I like doing it once in a while. I like how it makes the house smell all wholesome and rich. I like throwing handfuls of noodles into a big pot of simmering golden broth. I like tasting and adding a little more onion powder or just a sprinkle of Italian seasoning to make it interesting. I spent a happy Saturday afternoon that week making a big batch of chicken noodle soup to serve both family and party guests.

And those kids *loved* that soup. Most of them had second helpings, and the girl who had had her wisdom teeth extracted felt cared for, and my son said thank you and meant it. That was a day when the second mile was filled with rewards.

From that experience and others, I have distilled a few questions I now ask myself in order to determine if a given situation is a candidate for a second-mile effort. If I can answer yes to all three of these questions, I'll happily pull out all the stops.

1. Will it feed me in some way—creatively or emotionally or physically or socially?

2. Is it important to another person's well-being?

3. Can I honestly say that I have the time and money to pursue it?

Running my little drum-cookie episode through this diagnostic check, we can see immediately that it was ill-advised.

1. It didn't feed me in any sense; it depleted me.

2. The well-being of the kindergarten class was clearly not in jeopardy.

3. I did have the money, but I certainly didn't have the time to do that job.

By contrast, one year I received an assignment to come up with a great dinner-party idea for the adults in our ward. I was given a committee and a budget and several weeks in which to plan this activity. We settled on an Orient Express theme, and I had a blast creating special invitations to look like train tickets, menus written all in French, even tea towels with an "OE" embroidered in the corner for the young men who were to serve as waiters to drape over their arms. I cheerfully delegated the activity portion of the evening to another person so my group could concentrate on the food, and we had a small advance party a couple of weeks early to test our menu: vichyssoise, salad, roulade with vegetables, and strawberry shortcake.

The party was a huge success, and it brought our ward members closer together in friendship and fun. Yes, it was a lot of work, but I still have happy feelings when I think about that dinner. So, once again applying the questions:

1. Was I fed in some way? Multiple ways—creatively, socially, and emotionally.

2. Was it important to another person's well-being? I like to think it made a positive difference in our ward members' interaction with each other.

3. Did I have enough time and money to accomplish it? Yes.

Ding-ding-ding! We have a winner!

It might be useful to note that if you're ever in the position of delegating a task that you'd like to see some second-mile effort expended on, you'll likely be happier with the results if all three conditions can be met for the person who is taking on the assignment. You can also see that it's a precious few tasks that will meet all three criteria. This little checklist is kind of a nice, objective way to give yourself permission to relax about a job that may not need as much attention as you're trying to give it.

A final word about first and second miles: If you've

already gone the second mile in developing a relationship with someone, chances are you'll know that person well enough to be able to serve him or her more effectively in the first mile. Case in point: My visiting teaching partner called me one day to say that one of our women was having some struggles. She didn't need major help, but it seemed that a gesture of support might be in order. Because my partner knew of this woman's particular fondness for Turtle Pie, a signature ice-cream treat at a local restaurant, it was simple for us to go pick up a pie and drop it by to her. Twenty minutes and a couple of dollars were all it took to make her feel totally loved and supported—but only because my partner had taken the time previously to learn and take note of the things that would lift that woman's spirits.

Developing a relationship almost always fills all three criteria: it feeds you emotionally and socially, it's important in the other person's life as well, and it doesn't take money (although it usually requires quite an investment of time). May God grant us the discernment to put more of our efforts into people and fewer into things, and we'll all be in a lot better position to cope with life.

Create a Few Things That Can Be Counted On

When I was pregnant with our first child, a friend of mine in the office who was also pregnant undertook to teach me a simple crochet stitch with which I could make a baby blanket. My ineptitude was evident early on, but I persevered, and if the finished product was not exactly geometrically pleasing, it was nevertheless cozy and comforting, and it became our daughter's security blanket. She would in fact grab it by the edge and work her way around it until she came to her favorite corner, which stuck out at an odd angle because I kept losing stitches in the first few rows as I was getting the hang of turning at the ends. She would hold that corner up close to her face and suck her thumb, and I could take her anywhere and leave her with anyone as long as she had her blanket. It created an instant calmness in her.

When the time came that we had to put an end to the thumb sucking, it was clear that the only way to accomplish this was to throw away the blanket. So we did so, in a brave and very grown-up ceremony, and then we cried a little and read some books and had some dinner and went on with our lives. I found out years later that our poor little girl had sneaked out the next day to try to retrieve her blanket from the garbage, but it was covered with rotting food matter by then and she had to leave it.

What she didn't know was that I had trimmed off that favorite, misshapen corner to save for her scrapbook. When she was a teenager, I came upon it in a little-used drawer and showed it to her. She screamed in delight as her fingers found the exact right spot and pressed it to her face. I half expected her to pop her thumb in her mouth, but she didn't take it that far. Still, the old, familiar feelings were obviously there.

Some people would call such a thing a crutch. These are usually people who have no children of their own. Or maybe they never experienced for themselves how comforting it can be to have a little piece of the scary, uncertain world reserved as an island of safety, a "time-out" from having to deal with the challenges of growing up.

Not all of our children have latched on to tangible,

physical objects in this way. True, we had one son who became so attached to a certain baseball cap that his grandmother worried aloud that his ears were going to start growing out sideways from his head. (The cap sat right down on top of them and folded them over at about a ninety-degree angle.) She thought his constant wearing of that cap, day and night, might be akin to the old custom of binding a Chinese girl's feet. We assured her that his ears sprang back when we removed the cap to wash his hair, and he eventually grew unscathed out of that phase, as we knew he would.

For some of our other children, though, security was vested less in objects than in ritual. We put our older ones to bed every night with "ten pats," a quick patting on the back while counting to ten that was an instant signal to settle in. I had gathered some favorite lullabies by the time the younger ones came along, and for years they would ask me to come "sing them down" at bedtime. When they were old enough to go to school, I would send them out in the morning with the admonition, "Learn many useful things!" It became our shorthand for "I love you; do your best; see you tonight." Once when I had to leave before they did, in order to make it to a meeting at work, my son called as I went out the door, "Earn many useful dollars!"

I'm a big believer in the security of routines because I can identify so many things from my own childhood that to this day provide an almost instant sense of well-being. One such thing is string-quartet music. My parents are both accomplished musicians—in fact, they met and fell in love when they were both members of the Utah Symphony—and when their friends came over for the evening it was to play not bridge or poker but string quartets. I remember many nights drifting off to sleep with the sound of violins, viola, and cello floating up the stairs.

I can also close my eyes and almost feel every turn of the car in the last block or two before it would pull into the driveway of my childhood home. How many times did I ride home in the backseat, three-quarters asleep, willing the trip to last a little longer so I wouldn't have to climb out and get all "waked up" going in to the house? Or, if it wasn't such a sleepy night, my sister and I would watch for the moon, which was paradoxically waiting at the end of every cross-street as we drove past.

Many of our family's traditions were associated with holidays throughout the year. The first year of our marriage, my husband thought I was out of my mind because I insisted on coloring hard-boiled eggs for Easter. True, we had no children, but I simply wasn't ready to let go of that ritual. Mind you, I had a mother who was still hiding an Easter basket for me after I had left home for college. By then she had invested it with a sort of twisted humorous bent, however. I was home for Easter vacation, and on Sunday morning she announced that we were to look for our baskets by the item in the house that we most treasured. My youngest brother's was a snap; his was under the piano. I don't remember where the other brother found his—probably by the TV or out in the car. But I searched all over the house for mine. I just couldn't figure it out. Finally Mom said, "Where do you always go first when you visit?" My basket was in plain sight—on top of the refrigerator.

Traditions don't need to be elaborate to be appreciated. For example, my mother-in-law makes this fabulous clam dip with cream cheese and Worcestershire sauce and lemon juice and other good stuff, and there is a big bowl of it on the table at every family occasion. It's the first recipe the daughters-in-law have to ask for as they come into the family, and the babies are given tastes of it off of their fathers' fingers (minus the chunks of clam, of course) almost as soon as they leave the womb. I have been to only one family dinner in twenty-three years at which clam dip was not on the menu, and the protests from the boys (of whom there are seven when everyone is in town) were so vehement that you would have thought their mother was serving sautéed crickets or something. Thank goodness it's a fairly uncomplicated recipe that can be worked up quickly or made well in advance!

People clearly can become hidebound about their traditions, which probably isn't such a good idea if you're going to get married and have children and make other major changes in your life circumstances. My husband and I really lucked out when we got married because our families' Christmas traditions didn't clash. My extended family had always gotten together on Christmas Eve, and his had gathered on Christmas night, so we never had to negotiate where we would go. Not many couples escape this battle so easily.

What I did have to give up eventually as the years went by was my practice of fixing elaborate treats to give to all our neighborhood friends as Christmas gifts. One year I made twenty cookie trains for assorted loved ones, with cars crafted out of those flat, rectangular coconut bars and striped-shortbread wheels, filled with assorted colorful candies, and decorated, if I do say so myself, pretty darn artfully. Those trains were a hit. Our friends were happy to receive them, and I was happy to have made them.

But have you ever tried to fashion a cookie train with toddlers in the house? After about half an hour, when there's icing squirted all over the cupboards and all your train wheels have bites taken out of them and there are only three M&Ms left to fill the cargo car, you realize it's time to throw in the towel. No tradition is worth getting into a screaming match with your children—that defeats the purpose entirely. That year our friends didn't receive any Christmas remembrance from us. We did end up writing a little New Year's toast for each family and tying it around the neck of a bottle of sparkling cider and delivering them all on New Year's Eve. Now I just send Christmas cards—if I get around to it. I try instead to show my love with homemade treats delivered at different times throughout the year; that way it can be done one friend at a time, and it gives people a boost when they might need it more.

The point is to understand what traditions and routines and rituals are for. At heart, they're just a way of saying "I love you." As simple a ritual as leaving the cheese off part of the casserole because two of the kids don't like melted cheese can be a quiet demonstration of love: "I know you, what you like and don't like, and your needs are important to me." It's embarrassing, almost, how easily I can be bought for a bag of peanut M&Ms because it shows that my husband pays attention. Knowing someone's favorite candy is just one little point of connection, symbolic of a larger caring that is sort of priceless.

Of course, many traditions can and should be a lot more meaningful than shared sugar. In fact, it is evident from the way things are done in the Church that there is something truly important in the repetition of certain routines. I find a vast security in the knowledge that every Sunday I will hear the same sacrament prayers and partake of the same little piece of bread and tiny cup of water and feel the same peace and determination settling on my soul, week after week, year after year. Every time I go to the temple, I make the same covenants and feel the strength of the same promises from my Father in heaven. I have my own islands of safety in scriptures and favorite books and personal prayers and sacred music. These are "time-out" places where I can go to get a rest from meeting the challenges of mortality.

If the most important concepts of eternity are embedded in tradition and ritual, doesn't it seem sensible to take every advantage of rituals to create daily security and joy? Taking that thought a step further, some of the best possible rituals are the ones that are connected to those eternal anchors. I knew we were doing something right, for instance, when our seven-year-old son came into the kitchen one Sunday morning whining, "Mom, do I have to go to—" and then he cut himself off in the middle of the sentence, shook his head, and said, "I know, I know. This family goes to church on Sunday."

Where did that child learn that "this family goes to church on Sunday"? I certainly don't remember ever verbalizing it. Obviously, he had gotten that message from observing and participating in our family's practice of regular church attendance. At that moment, I was truly grateful that I had not succumbed to the temptation to just stay home until the children were older. It hadn't been easy to drag them over to a three-hour block of church every week, knowing that I would likely as not spend a good portion of the time chasing them down the halls, herding them to the bathroom and the drinking fountain, and nursing their baby siblings alone in the kitchen, sitting on a cold, metal chair. Many was the Sunday I stood over the counter in the restroom changing a diaper and thinking, "What is the *point?*"

But every Sunday we packed up the diaper bag and the quiet books and the pencils and paper. (I stopped taking cold cereal after I caught my son in the middle of a full-blown Lucky Charms war with the kid on the next bench, right in front of the podium.) Every Sunday we would at least put in an appearance in the chapel. We usually managed to last through the sacrament and sometimes, if we had 1:00 church and the baby fell asleep, we heard the first speaker as well. As we chose our pew, I used to greet the people behind us with a before-the-fact apology. *Surgeon General's Warning: Sitting behind this family can be hazardous to your attention.* I wasn't exactly getting spiritually fed in those days—or so I thought. But it was worth it to have our children know beyond a doubt that "This family goes to church on Sunday." And I have since learned that if you're doing what the Lord wants you to do, he makes up the difference when you miss out on other things.

He also seems to honor the intent of a righteous desire even if the execution is not always flawless. We try in our family to have scripture study before school, which makes for a pretty early morning when the oldest has to leave at 7:05. We achieve this goal with varying degrees of success. Sometimes the kids are fairly alert, and we get a good discussion going. Other times they stagger into the living room, wrapped in their blankets, and collapse on the couch, rousing themselves enough to read when it's their turn, but not apparently getting a whole lot out of the experience. I have often been surprised, though, when I have asked a gospel question and gotten an insightful answer from a child I thought was half asleep. They absorb more than I would ever have imagined, and it is especially important to them now to get in that prayer for our two missionaries before we start our day.

We are far from perfect. We miss a day here and there. Every now and then a child who doesn't have to go to school so early rolls over and moans and begs off, and we don't make a big deal out of it. Sometimes we're slow to get started and have time for only a verse or two. And we skipped over the whole Isaiah part of the Book of Mormon because it was bogging us down unmercifully and the kids weren't understanding it anyway (to say nothing of the parents). But "this family reads scriptures in the morning," and there is a peace in that idea that transcends all the imperfections in the mechanics of carrying it out.

The other tradition that has meant the most to our family over the years began in the early 1970s when my grandparents moved back to Utah after twenty-four years living in the East. One of the first things they did after they were settled in was to announce their intention to begin holding a Sunday evening "Family Gathering" of the sort my own father had attended at *his* grandmother's as a child. Any family members who were available would drop by anytime after 7:00 or so for a visit and a sweet roll. I was a young college student at the time, and Family Gathering was a convenient and simple way to keep in touch with my relatives. In fact, one of the things that attracted me about my husband-to-be was how well he fit in there, and we have attended regularly all our married life.

My grandparents have been gone for several years, but we still meet at my aunt's home. For well over two decades, Family Gathering has been the site for current-event discussions, piano and voice recitals, impromptu plays and puppet shows, and cousins' games. Out-of-town family members who are visiting over a Sunday can count on being able to see a good percentage of the extended family just by showing up. I have great relationships with most of my twenty-eight cousins, and my children know some of their second cousins better than most people know their firsts. When they take their first steps or get a part in the school play or bring home straight A's, they can generally count on twenty to forty people being there to cheer. And someday, when they find a boy or girl that they are thinking of marrying, I know one of the tests will be how well that person fits in at Family Gathering. Any prospective spouse who can survive that sort of scrutiny, I tell them, is worth looking at twice.

Not every family can have such a tradition, I realize. But anyone who feels a commitment can find things to do on a regular basis that will help children know who they are and how many people care about them. This sense of belonging, of being part of something stable and reliable and lasting, is the whole reason for creating traditions. Whether they're as simple as hot chocolate on Saturday mornings or as long-term as going to the temple twice a month, find the traditions that work for your family and you will find a great shield against the winds of uncertainty that blow unceasingly around us all.

Know When to Holler for Help

The first time my baby had a fever, I was extremely nervous about taking her temperature. There was no such thing as an ear thermometer in those days, except in the hospital, and the only way to get a reliable reading at home was with the good old rectal stick. I was sitting with the baby on my lap, the *Better Homes and Gardens Baby Book* propped open in front of me, trying to muster enough nerve to do the deed. Visions swam through my anxious brain of that little tube of glass snapping in half as I tried to get it to work, and every passing minute cemented further my conviction that we were going to end up in the hospital with both posterior lacerations and mercury poisoning.

In a state of near panic, I called my neighbor down the

street, a veteran mom, and she hurried right over. As she came in, she touched a wrist to the baby's forehead and said instantly, "Yup, she's got a fever, all right." I tendered the thermometer, and she gave it a couple of sharp, businesslike shakes with an obviously practiced hand. "Have you got any Vaseline?" she asked as she squinted at the slender silver line of mercury. I had to reply no. I don't understand to this day *why* I didn't have any Vaseline; I certainly had everything else that book had recommended was necessary for the well-equipped nursery. But no, I didn't have it.

"Okay," she improvised, "how about Crisco?"

"Like in the vegetable shortening?" I asked, dumbfounded.

"Sure," she said. "It's all natural, right?"

So I got a scoop of Crisco, and we dipped the end of the thermometer in it, and my friend showed me how to hold the baby on her stomach crosswise on my lap so I could keep a firm hold on both infant and thermometer, and we got the reading and were done with it. I was so relieved I was almost shaking; my neighbor, of course, was perfectly calm and helped me administer some Children's Tylenol and made up a bottle of diluted apple juice for the baby to keep her from getting dehydrated. I guess she was in my house for maybe fifteen minutes, but more than twenty years later I can still remember how grateful I was for her help.

This taught me a great lesson about accepting service that I have had to learn over and over again throughout my adult life because it's not something I'm good at. If I hadn't been desperate that one time, I probably wouldn't have called my neighbor—how embarrassing is it to admit that you don't even know how to take your baby's temperature? Blessed was I because I was compelled to be humble in that case, but how much more blessed would I be if I could be humble without being compelled? I have witnessed over and over again the amazing way in which doors are opened and bonds created when I'm willing to lay aside my pride and confess that there's something I can't do.

We hear all the time in the Church how important it is for us to give service, but we sometimes forget that in order for service to be rendered there must be a "servee" as well as a server. It's a grand scheme that provides for some to be given one gift and some another, that all may be profited thereby (see D&C 46:11–12). I had a moment of epiphany one day when I realized that if I couldn't let others serve me, I was in effect implying that their gifts weren't good enough for me. That puts a different spin on things!

So now I'm willing to admit cheerfully that there are many things I don't do well, and that makes me twice as grateful for those who *are* capable in those areas. Unfortunately, there seems to be a little handful of talents that "play well" in church, and if you're a good speaker or teacher or can sing in sacrament meeting, people assume you're more gifted than they are, whereas if sacrament meeting involved getting grass stains out of jeans or Dutch-oven cooking or changing a tire they would see how helpless you can be. I wish we had more opportunities to really appreciate each other's contrasting competencies.

One of my own areas of complete idiocy is camping. I was not raised to camp. In my family of origin, "roughing it" meant drawing the short straw and having to sleep on the roll-away cot at the Holiday Inn. So it was with some trepidation that I agreed, the year I was a Mia Maid adviser, to attend rough camp with our Young Women. This involved sleeping bags, rolled out in tents that we had pitched ourselves, and food cooked without an oven, and toilet provisions much too primitive to enumerate.

As capable as my imagination was of stirring up the worst possible scenarios, nothing I had envisioned approached even remotely the misery of that first night of rough camp. I suppose the fact that there were still pockets of snow in the shady areas of the campsite might have tipped me off, but I didn't expect the biting, merciless, hideously cold wind that blew through the tent—not in one long blast but at frequently recurring intervals that announced themselves with a wild, whooshing sound through the pine trees before they hit. I began to feel a rush of despair every time that noise started up; listening to the approach of a pack of wolves could scarcely have been more intimidating.

I was huddled in the fetal position in my sleeping bag, shaking uncontrollably, my double-stockinged feet two blocks as solid and cold as a gangster's cement overshoes, when I heard seven words I hope never to hear again as long as I draw breath: "Emily, I threw up in the tent."

I will admit that I said several very un-Young-Women-like words to myself as I dragged my body out of my freezing sleeping bag into the even more frozen air at 2:00 A.M. and called softly through the wall of the tent to April, our camp director, who was in the next tent over. When I told her in a stage whisper what had happened, I could distinctly hear her start to giggle. "There are paper towels in the back of the truck," she offered once she had gotten control of herself.

There was no choice. I zipped myself out of the tent into the harsh night, hoisted my leaden feet onto the back bumper of the truck, and stood in the gale-force winds rummaging under a stiff canvas tarp until I blessedly hit upon a roll of paper towels. There was already a garbage bag hanging in a nearby tree, so I grabbed that, and we wiped up the mess as well as we could by flashlight and put the bag outside and went back to "sleep."

The next morning, when the reveille bugle roused me to a half-conscious state, I heard April telling the girls not to wake me. "She had a rough night," she said. I thought I detected a little of the previous night's amusement in her voice, but I was too tired to tell for sure.

There was enough sun by then to bring the temperature up to a bearable level in the tent, so I stayed in there for another hour or so, emerging to find that April had worked magic with a pile of potatoes and cheese and eggs and bacon in two large Dutch ovens. If we had had to rely on *my* skill for our breakfast that morning, we would have all been eating boiled pine cones. Do you think it occurred to me at that moment to be jealous of her capability? Do you think I resented the fact that she could do something I couldn't? No way!

When we truly need each other, we can rejoice in each other's skills rather than competing or feeling threatened. The first step to that is the hardest—we have to admit our need.

One of the things I love about the Church is that it gives us lots of opportunities to serve and lots of opportunities to need other people's service. There was a good deal of amusement in my ward the year I was called to head up the humanitarian service project. We had been asked to provide 250 newborn kits for the humanitarian center—kits that included, among other things, a layette gown, a receiving blanket, and a pair of booties. There was no way we could afford to buy all those things; we were going to have to sew the bulk of them. And, as I have mentioned previously, everyone in my Relief Society was intimately acquainted with my inadequacies as a seamstress. I needed help, and a lot of it.

I spent more time that year in fabric shops than I had in the previous twenty years combined. I told the sisters that if the spirit of Elijah was what spurred one on to do family history work, I surely must have gotten the spirit of Bernina, because I was suddenly acutely aware of the price of flannel and could almost smell it in the air when fleece went on sale.

What I couldn't do in the sewing department, I made up for by washing fabric to shrink it, as well as ironing it and cutting it to the proper size. Then I cast those bundles of fabric upon the waters, as it were, and after not too many days they came back to me as beautiful finished blankets for our project.

A woman in the ward found us a cute and easy pattern for booties that could be made out of fleece, so we did a lot of those. In addition, several sisters with fabulous skills spent hours knitting and crocheting, and they turned out the most darling creations! I know that the people who got those newborn kits must have felt like someone really cared about them.

That project was a perfect example of the blessings that result when people need each other. I'll always be grateful for the things I learned about hollering for help and treasuring other people's gifts.

Apparently this has been a lesson I have needed, because when my husband and I decided several years ago, after much discussion and prayer, that I would go back to work full time, it took me many months to acknowledge that I could no longer do everything that I had been accustomed to doing around the house. I was running myself ragged trying to prove that I could balance the two roles and do it all. One day my husband looked deep into my eyes and said, "You know, I'm perfectly capable of going to the grocery store." Well, of course he was. But did he know what brand of tuna fish to buy, and how to pick a decent cantaloupe, and how to save money on taco mix?

No, he didn't know all that, not at first. Nor did my young teens know how to do their own laundry—not because they weren't capable of doing it but because it honestly had never even occurred to me to try to teach them. I had been perfectly happy to do it for them and saw it, I think, as a way of showing my love for them. But when my housekeeping time was suddenly severely curtailed, and clean underwear and socks became a scarcity, Dad simply took the kids into the laundry room and showed them how to work the machines, and that was that. Thank goodness it happened in time for my children to be seasoned laundry veterans by the time they left on their missions!

Now when I throw in a load of laundry for the kids it's a bonus, a favor, instead of something they just expect to have happen. Our children are much more independent and helpful than they were when I was the "boss," and they have more control over their own lives. If they want clean socks, they know what to do; they don't have to wait until Mom gets around to it.

I had a bishop tell me, when I was Relief Society president in our ward, that it was up to me to be training my replacement, and that if I didn't learn to delegate, I would have to do this job for the rest of my life. It didn't occur to me at the time that the same principle applied in my family. If I didn't teach those kids to scrub the toilet, not only would I have to do it for the rest of my life but it would become one more thing for them to fight over with their spouses someday.

Delegating tasks, at home or at church, never came easily to me. I get in my mind the way I want something done, and it's hard to turn it over to somebody else to execute. And I don't think it's ever easy to get little children to pitch in, especially when it comes to picking up their toys. I had one small son who would collapse on the floor whenever I asked him to help out, screaming, "My legs don't work! My legs are broken! I can't move!" There's no question that it's usually just way easier to do the thing yourself.

I was filled with admiration, though, when my sons

had some friends over for a sleep over and those boys, ages ten and eight, carried their own dishes to the sink after breakfast. I could almost hear their mother saying to them hundreds, maybe thousands, of times: "Clear your places, please. Take your dishes to the sink, please. Could you please come get your plate and take it to the sink?" (Or, maybe more realistically, "Get in here now and get your dishes off the table!") Anyway, the training had sunk in with these boys, and it made me wish I had stuck with my own efforts a little better. We have improved in our later years, but not without pain.

These lessons are blessings to our family that we may never have received had I not been *forced* to acknowledge my need for help. I have wondered if part of the reason we felt good about my going back to work was because of my children's need to become more self-sufficient. This is not to say that this is the solution to anyone else's problems. There were many factors in our family's situation that made it a good choice for us. We tried to keep foremost in our minds the governing principle that the eternal welfare of our family would always be our greatest concern. Once we accepted that as the "given," we seemed to find a lot of flexibility in the way we achieved that goal of a healthy family.

For example, now that we're both working, my husband starts at his job earlier in the morning so he can be home when the children finish school. I stay home later to get them off to school and then work later in the afternoon. We try to have a parent available at all times, but we don't sweat which parent that will be. Our answers have grown out of our needs, and they have always been forthcoming when we have been honest about what we have needed.

I remember once watching my two-year-old son, who was in that stubborn, I'll-do-it-myself phase, trying to put on his own pajamas. They were the one-piece, footed style of sleepwear, and he got them all twisted around and bunched up and in just a terrible mess. Every couple of minutes I would reach out a hand, but he kept slapping me away. I finally left him to it and went into the kitchen to work. A few minutes later he was at my side, head bowed, holding up his limp pajamas. I hugged him and helped him into them and bundled him off to bed with his favorite lullabies and ten extra pats on top of the traditional ten.

I see myself from time to time as that little boy, struggling and fighting with some situation in my life and making a twisted mess of things, unwilling to surrender control to One who could easily help me resolve the problem and send me happily on my way. An institute teacher comes to mind, one who used to look us in the eye and say, "Ere you left your room this morning, did you . . . ?"

He who knows our needs stands ready to help us fulfill them, but we have to ask. May pride never keep us from acknowledging our deficiencies to him. May we stand ready to help one another, and to accept each other's gifts of love and service. Most of all, may we acknowledge and accept the sacrifice of our Savior, who truly did for us what we could not do for ourselves.

Factor In What's Playing in the Background

Our fourth child was a perfectly amiable toddler who could amuse himself for long stretches of time with a spoon, a bowl, and a tablespoon of Cheerios. So I got particularly exasperated with him one day when he seemed unnaturally grouchy and clingy. He whined to be held, but when I picked him up he got squirmy and irritated. He followed me around the house, plucking at my pant leg and trying to get my attention the whole morning. I finally spoke a little more sharply to him than I was accustomed to doing, but I had things I needed to do and he just wasn't cooperating. I was never so relieved for nap time to come!

You can imagine my remorse when I went in later to pick him up from his nap and found that he was running a raging fever. He hadn't been purposely trying to drive me crazy all morning; he was sick! I was so sorry that I had been too preoccupied to pick up on the signals he was sending me that something was out of kilter that day.

The truth is, taking into account just the seven people in our immediate family, not to mention the friends and relatives on the near periphery, it's a rare day when everything is *in* kilter for everyone. It's fairly easy to cut a little child some slack—he's hungry, he needs a nap, he's cutting teeth, we've been dragging him around all day and he's just worn out. Why can't we do that for each other, or, even rarer, for ourselves?

The example that always comes to mind is the person, male or female, who cuts me off in traffic. There's a reason why road rage is such a serious issue: there are a lot of seemingly selfish drivers out there. I like to make up stories for why the person must be in such an all-fired hurry. The more far-fetched the story, the better I feel. Some possible scenarios:

1. This man and his wife have tried for seven years to have a child. She finally got pregnant, and she was sick, sick, sick, but they hung in there for the whole nine months, and now she has just called from the hospital: "I'm having the baby! Get here quick!"

2. Or the girl's parents sold their television to buy the dress she has to wear in the finals of the Miss Taylorsville pageant, and the dress is at the cleaner's, which closes in five minutes.

3. Maybe the somewhat shy older man has been corresponding on the Internet with the girl of his dreams, and they've agreed to meet at last, and his boss kept him in a meeting for an extra half-hour and if he doesn't get to the restaurant soon she will just leave, feeling stranded and betrayed, and he'll never get her back.

You get the idea. The great thing is that if you can get yourself lost in an outlandish story, pretty soon you forget all about your frustration over being cut off on the freeway. At the very least, you can remind yourself that you have no idea what's playing in the background of the offender's life at the moment. Assume it was just a mistake, and don't let it ruin your day.

Speaking of ruined days, do you ever have days when you feel as if you could just pop someone right in the nose for no particular reason? There are times when it seems like every nerve in my body is standing straight on its edge. (Do nerves even have edges? Is that why we say we're feeling "edgy"?) On such a day, if the dog is barking when I come home, just as he does every day of his little dog life, it is all I can do to refrain from booting him across the yard. Children wander innocently into the kitchen and ask what's for dinner, and I launch into a tirade, "Why can't I ever just come into the house and take off my stupid panty hose and relax for five seconds without you jumping my case about your precious dinner?" I see them telegraphing each other with their eyebrows—kid code for "Lie low! Mom's on one!" My husband looks up as I slam into the bedroom to shed my work clothes, and he says knowingly, "Uh-oh. What's the date?" And *that* infuriates me no end, to think that he so glibly dismisses my perfectly legitimate bad mood by attributing it to a hormonal imbalance.

Even more infuriating is that he is almost always right! Countless times I have traced my most unreasonable behavior straight to its hormonal source, and yet still I find myself surprised month after month when it flares up again. I know I need to learn to recognize the warning signs and just roll with it, trying not to take it out on the kids or the dog or the spouse. Most of all, I need to remember not to succumb to the guilt that always assails me when I am awash in seemingly uncontrollable negative feelings.

If you've ever been wave-jumping in the ocean, you

know that every so often a really big one comes and throws you off your feet. When that happens, you're more likely to get hurt if you panic and flail around. It's better just to grab a deep breath, curl up, and ride it out. You'll get to shore all right, brush yourself off, and wade back out—because most of the time it's a lot of fun to jump through the waves. It's worth the risk of an occasional bump or bruise.

Life is full of big waves, and at any given time you or someone you know is probably being swept to shore, being dragged along on the sandbars and sputtering with a noseful of seawater. Cut them some slack. Cut yourself some slack. Be patient until you can get your feet under you, and if you need to, get out for a little while and lie on the beach before you venture back into the water.

There are waves, and then there are undercurrents. The virtue of having a subconscious mind is that it can process multiple emotions that would be too overwhelming if they were all bouncing around in our conscious minds—we would never get anything done. But the downside is that things can pile up, and after a while we can find ourselves being bothered beyond measure by such petty annoyances as a toothpaste glob in the sink or a stray sock lost in the laundry.

Every now and then I hit a night when I just can't sleep, and the responsibilities and frustrations of the day cycle themselves around and around in my brain. On one such night, I got up, took a notebook into the living room, and started making a list of my concerns. I wrote down everything that came into my mind: The horrible, grinding noise the new refrigerator was making. The Relief Society lesson I had to prepare for Sunday. The groceries I hadn't gotten around to buying yet. The war in Afghanistan. The pile of papers waiting for my attention at work. The insect collection my son had to do for his biology class. The letter from our missionary son saying someone had given anti-Mormon literature to their most promising investigator. The faltering economy.

That list went on for quite a while, and I thought as I read it over, "No wonder I'm such a grouch!" Then into my mind came the words of the "serenity prayer" that is often recited in Alcoholics Anonymous and other twelve-step groups, which goes something like this: "God, grant me the serenity to accept the things I cannot change, the courage to change the things I can, and the wisdom to know the difference." So, saying a little prayer for wisdom, I went down my list and put a *C* (for *change*) by the things I thought I could actually do something about, and an

S (for *serenity*) next to the ones over which I had no control. It was surprising how many *C*s there actually ended up being, and how minor those problems seemed when I yanked them up out of my subconscious and plastered them down in black and white. My life wasn't nearly as unmanageable as I had thought. I just needed to look it right in the face and get on with it.

I have wondered since that night if maybe one of Satan's cleverest tactics might be to keep us so busy with our everyday messes that problems pile up in our subconscious minds and weigh us down. We can't deal with them unless we bring them up to the level of consciousness. So we keep dragging along, never quite knowing what is wrong, never quite feeling caught up, never budgeting any of our energy for the things that are playing in the background.

Mothers in particular seem to get caught in this trap because we're so often unused to consulting our own feelings. We focus instead on how everyone else is doing, striving to juggle the emotions of the entire family. We get to the breaking point and don't even know we're there because we're so wrapped up in keeping all the balls in the air.

In one especially trying season of my life, my husband

suggested that I needed a night off every week just to do what I wanted, and so he would be taking over on Wednesday evenings and I was to leave the house. Imagine my astonishment that first Wednesday when I couldn't think of a single thing to do! In my well-meaning efforts to see that my family had everything they needed, I had completely lost track of my own needs and desires and interests. Every mother makes sacrifices, of course, but there is a point where this can become counter-productive. You can't give of yourself if you have no self to give.

On that first "night off" I found myself at the mall. I wandered around for a while and then I just sat down on a bench and thought. What did I want? What did I like? What would feed me in this precious two or three hours? I ended up going in my mind clear back to my college years, my single days, when money may have been scarce but my time was my own. I gradually remembered little things that I had enjoyed: a particular kind of pen I liked to write with; a spot in the downtown public library where I used to sit with a book I'd picked off a shelf; an old music album I had loved listening to. Bit by bit, I began to rediscover that part of me that I had brought to the making of this marriage and family in the first place.

It didn't happen all on that first night. But as the weeks progressed, and I brought more of that self home with me each time, I learned that I had greater gifts to give my family than clean socks and hot meals. I was reminded of the Savior's indictment of the rule keepers of his day: "Woe unto you, scribes and Pharisees, hypocrites! for ye pay tithe of mint and anise and cummin, and have omitted the weightier matters of the law, judgment, mercy, and faith: these ought ye to have done, and not to leave the other undone" (Matthew 23:23). Woe unto me, who had gotten caught up in the minutia of removing stains and disguising ground beef and cleaning the lint filter, and had neglected the weightier matters of mothering: nurturing and listening and teaching. Those ought I to have done— and not to leave the other undone. Stains need to be removed, after all, and if you don't clean out that lint filter you'll be sorry by and by. But those are the little things you do to make the true job of being the Mom run more smoothly. They aren't the job themselves. They aren't the "weightier matters."

In that period of my life, I learned the importance of creating your own background as a mother, so that when the stuff in the foreground comes rushing at you like a tidal wave, you can handle it. The key to this is knowing who you are and then bringing that person, well and whole, to the mothering party.

Inevitably, prayer is going to play a big role in the process. After all, "who you are" goes back a lot further than this tiny slice of eternity we call mortality. If you want to understand the deepest part of yourself, who better to stay in touch with than the One who knows that part better than anyone—better than you yourself know it? When you are comfortable with your spirit, you can go forward armed with powerful spiritual tools instead of the flimsy hardware you might accumulate in the world.

You get comfortable with your spirit just the way you might get comfortable with a person who becomes a good friend—by spending time with it, attending to it, learning from it, recognizing its needs, and appreciating it. You have to feed it to keep it healthy, and a steady diet of scriptures and service works nicely, with maybe some good music and family fun for dessert. If you make your spirit sick with entertainment that you know better than to involve yourself in, or simply starve it to death through neglect, you won't ever be happy with it. And if you're unhappy with your spirit, you're unhappy with yourself in the most fundamental way.

When we were newlyweds, my husband's parents gave

us a beautiful set of very sharp kitchen knives. I, who had grown up in a household with mostly dull knives, protested at first. I was a little frightened, frankly; it seemed as if you could chop off a finger as readily as a carrot-end. But I soon learned that sharp knives are actually safer to use than dull ones if you pay attention to how you use them, primarily because you don't have to seize the food in a death grip in order to keep it in place while you saw away at it. Now it drives me crazy to work with a dull knife.

Similarly, I know lots of people who don't seem to want to be spiritually sharp. They're afraid of cutting themselves off from the fun of life. Sawing away at worldly pursuits, they blunt their spiritual edges and render themselves less able to do what matters most. Their background becomes a buzz-saw of discontent as they seek more powerful tools for coping with life, never realizing that they're shopping at the wrong hardware store. It's a tragic but all-too-common mistake.

Another common mistake, one that afflicts mothers probably more than anyone else, is the assumption we tend to make that we are responsible not just for our own backgrounds but for everyone else's as well. How often have we heard that the mother sets the tone in the home?

It's true that we can have a lot of influence on our family's environment, but "setting the tone" does not necessarily equate with "being responsible for the moods of everyone." If you've ever spent the morning with a child who got up grouchy and deteriorated from there, you know that sometimes people feel crummy in spite of their mothers' best efforts. You can drive yourself crazy trying to shake a child loose of a bad mood, or you can recognize that there might be something playing in the background of that person's life that has nothing to do with you, and stop feeling like it's your fault that he or she isn't deliriously happy every waking moment.

It's always more productive to concentrate your energy on the elements of your life that might possibly be within your control. By and large, other people's moods won't fall into that category. What you *can* control is your response to those moods, so that you don't contribute to the clutter in the person's background and make things even more difficult. Sometimes a judicious separation of parties is in order—the blessed time-out system. (By the time you're the Mom, a time-out is actually more of a reward than a punishment!) Sometimes a quiet word or a little note can help calm the turmoil. If a listening ear seems called for, you can offer it. What you cannot do is solve the person's problem by doing the work that he or she needs to do in order to arrive at a solution. What you provide will be a temporary fix at best, an impediment to true resolution at worst.

I learned this the hard way on child number one. (Sometimes I marvel at the miracle it is that she has arrived at adulthood intact.) Because I felt responsible for everything about her life, I was deeply invested in her schoolwork, feeling that if she got a bad grade it would reflect on me. She got fairly adept in elementary school at putting off a project until the last minute, then coming to me in tears to have me pick up the pieces and do most of the work myself. In fairness to her, I don't think she did this on purpose. It was a product of my having trained her that I could do the work better and faster than she could (duh!) and that she didn't really have to measure up because I would bail her out rather than let "us" fail.

I thought I was bolstering my daughter's self-image by helping her get good grades. But a wise friend taught me that what I was *really* doing was teaching her that she wasn't smart enough to do her work herself. Some self-image boost, huh? One of the hardest feats I accomplished that year was to step back when she belatedly brought me a big project and to say, "Gosh, honey, that seems like a problem. What are your plans for fixing it?" I think she got a C- on that project, but every point she did earn was her own. More important, every point she missed was her own lost opportunity, and she eventually started taking responsibility for those points as well.

Fortunately, children are pretty resilient, and as long as there's lots of love playing in the background, most of our parenting mistakes can be absorbed into the mix without doing too much damage. As we learn to be gentler with each other, to cut each other some slack, and to have better control over our own personal environments, our footing will be sure and we will survive any wave that comes.

If It Can Be Vacuumed Up, Wiped Off, or Washed Out, Don't Worry about It

When, in our second year of marriage, we took possession of our first house, we spent our earliest moments in it walking from room to room, basking in the feeling of our own space and choosing where we would put our things. The place was immaculate and welcoming, but we got a good laugh when we went down to the basement and found, in the large family room, a box of Cheerios square in the middle of the floor, about half its contents scattered around on the carpet. What better way could there have been to announce that this was a house for children?

Several months later, when we brought our first baby home to that house, we might as well have fired off a gun and announced, "Let the mess begin!" It wasn't long before we learned how low on the disaster spectrum a few handfuls of Cheerios would fall. Dry cereal—a mountain of it—has nothing on a single renegade Fruit Loop that slips unnoticed from a child's bowl into a corner and congeals there, adhering itself in a semipermanent bond with the linoleum. Of course, before you even evolve to the Fruit Loop stage, you've got the Age of Rice Cereal, a concoction for infants that is frequently compared—and with just cause—to wallpaper paste. When our baby was first learning to eat solid foods, she couldn't swallow a bite of anything without poking her thumb in her mouth, and when a child shoves a thumb into a mouthful of rice cereal and then waves her hands around, the entire room gets a good plastering.

And it just escalates from there. Unless you handcuff the child to you for the next several years, that kid is going to find a way to be alone enough to make a lot of glorious messes. Of course, the best messes are always made by unsupervised children. You might leave them for five minutes, playing happily with a roomful of toys, so you can seize the opportunity to make a quick phone call. Then just as you are starting to relax into the calm of an adult conversation, the realization dawns that it may be a little *too* quiet. Either the child has fallen asleep on the floor, or havoc is being wrought. It is usually the latter. Hang up the phone quickly and find out.

I've been pretty lucky in this regard. I had only one child out of five take scissors to her hair, and even then it was a relatively restrained snip. None of them were interested in pills or toxic substances. They did like to pull all the books off the bookshelf, but that's no big deal. We had one episode with blue marker all over a two-year-old's stomach, but it wasn't a permanent marker. My philosophy is that if you are going to insist on bringing a permanent marker into a household with small children, you are asking for trouble and deserve what you get.

Rolling the toilet paper off the roll was a favorite pastime of my toddlers, and they liked to splash in the toilet, although they rarely threw things into it. Once we left the baby in her infant seat on the kitchen table when the front doorbell interrupted our dinner, and when we got back thirty seconds later she had smeared sour cream all over her legs like body lotion. Mmmm, smooth! And we had our share of babyglyphics on the wall, although nothing like a friend of mine whose son finally turned to writing on his walls with White-Out so he wouldn't get caught so soon.

All of those things were exasperating, but we soon

learned that they weren't worth fretting about. I, for one, do not have enough spare emotional energy to be expending it on things that aren't going to matter a whit by next week. And so if a mess gets made, we clean it up. We try to get the mess-maker to take a hand in the cleaning, if possible, but if sometimes that doesn't work out, we just do it ourselves and have done with it.

I feel so sorry for mothers who think that a mess is a personal indictment of their homemaking skills. I'm not advocating living in squalor, you understand, but life is a messy business, and if you don't get dirty once in a while, you're probably not really in the game. I'll never forget an evening when we had some friends and their children over for movies and popcorn. We turned on the lights at the end of the show to find quite a little blizzard left on the floor, especially in the vicinity of the popcorn bowl. Our friends immediately began apologizing, and I just waved them off, saying, "That's what vacuum cleaners are for." Their mouths dropped open, and the husband turned to his wife and said, "Did you hear that?" I'm guessing (and it's an educated guess because I know what that family's house looks like whenever I step into it) that such an incident in their home might have been considered a capital crime. Think of how much fun you miss out on if you spend your life worrying about popcorn getting scattered!

The truth is, people are less interested than you think in the dust bunnies under your bed. I have a friend who called me all in a tizzy one day because, she said, her visiting teachers had come and she just knew they were looking at the corners of her ceilings and gossiping to the whole ward about her failure as a housekeeper. If I thought my visiting teachers or anyone else who came into my house gave two figs about the corners of my ceilings, I would have to shut myself off from all polite company for the rest of my life. I choose not to do that.

Now, I'm the first to admit that I'm a pretty crummy housekeeper. No—I'm the second to admit it; my husband would be the first. But I can tackle a pile that would send my cleaner friends to bed for a week. I'm better at making large, heroic efforts than smaller, consistent ones. If I want to have someone over, I clean as much as I reasonably can in the time allotted and then throw the rest into the closets and shut the doors. That's what closet doors are for, you know. I don't want to miss the opportunity for pleasant interaction due to my imperfections as a homemaker. And, interestingly enough, I still seem to have friends, and they still seem willing to come in my house, so I guess I'm doing all right.

If only the messes of life were restrained to physical things! Emotional messes are every bit as prevalent and can consume even more energy unnecessarily if we let them. They're harder to shake off, but we have to learn to do it or we will be consumed by them, because they are a huge part of life. It's a real skill to be able to simply clean up after ourselves and move on.

I'm not talking about deep-seated emotional problems here. Those are obviously more serious and need true attention. I'm talking about the little annoyances of every-day life that can eat us up if we let them. Traffic tickets, for example. One day I got two tickets in the space of three hours because I was hurrying to drop off a child at preschool and then to pick him up afterward, and I didn't recognize the flash of the Photo-Cop radar system. What a pain! What a waste of money! What an adding of insult to injury, because the reason I was rushing in the first place was that the preschooler's baby sister was ill, and I had to squeeze in a trip to the pediatrician between the drop-off time and the pickup time.

Even worse was the day I was walking across Main Street in Salt Lake City. They were laying the TRAX line, so there was a big island in the middle of the road, and it was a common practice for people to go straight across from the store entrance on the west side of the street to the store entrance on the east side rather than walk half a block down to the crosswalk. I looked left, found the way clear, and crossed to the middle of the street. Then I looked right—right into the face of two motorcycle policemen who were stationed at the crosswalk. Now what? Should I turn around and run back into Mervyn's? Stand there like an idiot for half an hour? Walk down the median strip to the crosswalk? No, I had already committed the deed, so I finished it off and crossed the rest of the way, hearing the motorcycle engine kick up a few decibels as the officer drove up behind me. That was a $58 ticket for an innocent little offense that endangered no one. You'd think he could have given me a warning, but no, he was there for his pound of flesh and he extracted it. (No residual bitterness here, as you can see.)

We are not a rich family, and we have at least five essential uses for every $58 that comes our way. So it is particularly galling to have to shell out money like that because of a stupid mistake. But after I had whined about it for a few weeks, my husband finally said, "You did it. You paid for it. Get over it." And of course, he was right.

I wasn't going to get the money back, and somehow we had managed to buy groceries and keep the electricity coming into our house in spite of it. Why insist on continuing to muddy my life with a mess that had already been cleaned up?

I've had plenty of occasion to beat myself up over self-made messes, and I'm trying to learn not to do it anymore. I can't help it that I make mistakes, but I can refrain from agonizing over them long after the damage has been essentially repaired. I'm remembering another really stupid thing I did once that cost me a lot more in emotional reserves than it cost our family in actual dollars. I had ordered a darling outfit from a catalog, a short-sleeved, pink, seersucker dress that looked utterly cool and summery and comfortable on the model. When the package arrived, I opened it with great anticipation and hurried into my room to try the dress on. Regrettably, the effect in real life did not bear any resemblance to the catalog representation. In the dress that had been so adorable on the model, I looked vaguely like a pregnant strawberry. It had hit the catalog model mid-calf, but on my six-foot frame it barely brushed my knees. I can't enumerate all the ways in which that dress was unsuitable; suffice it to say it was a huge disappointment. I quickly bundled it back into its packing materials and set it aside to mail back.

And forgot it.

When, six months later, I came upon that package that I still had not returned, I was mortified. I didn't think the company would even take it back by then, and, frankly, I was too embarrassed to call and find out. So that dress sat accusingly in my room for another six months because I was paralyzed with guilt over having made a bad buying decision in the first place and then escalating the stupidity by failing to get a refund. I kept thinking I'd get up nerve enough to call the company. Then I would chicken out, reasoning that they probably didn't even carry that dress anymore, that it was out of season, that they would think I was nuts.

This went on until the happy day I took a tour of the Church's humanitarian center, and it occurred to me that although I couldn't use the dress, somewhere in the world there was a woman who would be thrilled to have it. I took it to Deseret Industries at once, picturing in my mind the glee of the person who would scoop up the bargain: "Look, honey, this looks like it's hardly even been worn!" It was gone. I was free. The mess had been cleaned up at last. I only wonder now why it took me so long to figure that one out. I've decided that the guilt factor is a major player in the messes of my life.

That being the case, it's always a huge relief when someone exercises charity and refrains from adding more guilt to the burden I already feel. My husband is a great man in this regard. He never makes me feel like an idiot, even when I have been one.

There was the time, for instance, when I was pregnant and tired and running behind, and I was supposed to pick him up at work, but I had to go to the bank first. I was driving a big old Ford station wagon we had inherited from his parents, the car of his childhood, and I didn't have the dimensions figured out all that well yet. To my dismay, as I pulled into the bank's drive-through, I heard a horrendous scraping noise on the passenger's side. Sure enough, there was a steel pillar there and I had scraped against it. But the car was old, and had no aesthetic value anyway, and so I shrugged it off and completed my errand and went to collect my husband.

When we came out of his office to go home, he reached to open my car door for me, then stopped short and asked thoughtfully, "How do you propose we get into the car?" I had apparently not just scratched the side of the station wagon but shorn the door handles completely off, front and back. He stood there quietly for a minute, and then he just started to laugh. We laughed and laughed, and we have laughed many times since, and he never made me feel awful for messing up that car although it was perfectly clear that I had acted with unsurpassed cluelessness in that incident. That is charity.

Contrast that with how you feel when other people seem bent on making mountains out of your molehills. I'm thinking of the year our ward had reserved a canyon campground for an overnight stay, and we were each supposed to bring our own picnic dinner. I had gone to the grocery store for our stuff, and right inside the front door there was a big display of a brand-new product, Cherry Coke, just out on the market. It was being offered at an introductory price, and I thought it would be fun to try, so I threw it in the basket.

We joined our ward family at the appointed hour, and after laying out the sandwich fixings and the chips and the olives, I pulled the Cherry Coke out of the cooler. You would have thought I had plunked down a six-pack of Bud Lite on that table. It got suddenly quiet, then I heard a few mothers whispering to their kids, and the bishop gave me kind of an amused look, as if to say, "You might have known better."

I'm not particularly proud of the fact that I have a Coke now and then, but I don't feel especially guilty about it either. To me, it's a molehill. I found out later, somewhat to my delight, that some people were so shocked at seeing me with a Coke in my hand that they thought I ought to be released as Relief Society president. I'm telling you here and now, if drinking Coke could really get a person out of being Relief Society president, I know one company whose stock would soar.

I didn't feel guilty about drinking Coke at the ward campout. However, I *did* feel rotten about having taken several mothers in my ward who were trying to live a "higher law" and put them in the position of needing to explain to their children why their Relief Society president could drink Coke and they couldn't. The bishop was right: I should have known better—not because I believed there was anything inherently sinful about what I had done but because it was potentially offensive to people I cared about. "Wherefore, if meat make my brother to offend, I will eat no flesh while the world standeth, lest I make my brother to offend" (1 Corinthians 8:13).

It's hard, though, to clean up a mess when others seem determined to stir it around. I hope I have learned in my years as a mother not to be judgmental when a fellow mom seems to be in a tough spot. I hope I know enough about the messiness of mortality to err on the side of mercy rather than justice. And I think I've learned enough to pick my battles with my own kids and not escalate the conflict just because someone else's knickers are in a twist.

When our sixteen-year-old son came home one day with bleached hair, for example, I cried a little. His friends had been experimenting with their hair for months, and I had taken some motherly pride in the fact that he had resisted, seeming to be above such folly. His bleached hair squelched that smugness pretty effectively.

Once I got over the initial jolt, though, I was quickly reconciled to the situation. Yes, as it started to grow out, I thought he looked like an ungroomed porcupine, but a trip to the high school confirmed that this was the way even nice boys looked at that time of their lives, and I probably didn't have anything much to worry about.

His peers didn't give him any grief, obviously, but *our* friends were a different story. The reactions were unexpectedly volatile: "Did you just *die* when you saw him?" "How could you let him do that to himself?" "I'll bet it broke your heart." Well, no, actually. It was a twinge, not a heartbreak, and I'm clearly still alive and willing to acknowledge my relationship with the child, and *hair grows out,* for goodness' sake! That's what I wanted to scream. What I did say, with exceeding calm and restraint, was "We think he's old enough to be accountable for his decisions. We're grateful that he chooses to make his statement of adolescent independence in a relatively inoffensive, nonpermanent way."

Honestly! What if that child had committed some *real* sin? This awakened in me a horrible thought: How many times have I, with my judgmental attitude, impeded another person's progress or diminished someone else's capacity to repent? How many times have I failed to see the whole picture and insisted on painting one little corner of it in the wrong colors? How many clever but hurtful comments have I insisted on making over the years that have created unnecessary stumbling blocks?

Next time I see a mess in someone's life—including my own—I hope I'll be less inclined to stand back and cluck my tongue and more willing to get in there with a bucket and a mop to help. And once something has been cleaned up, I hope I can do better at going on with life and never wasting another thought on it!

Accept Life as a Glorious Adventure Full of Gifts for You

A few years ago, we acquired a miniature schnauzer, one of those canine breeds that I have always categorized as Little Yappy Dogs. I had never had much use for LYDs up to that time, but this dog, whom we named Toby, is so affectionate and so patient and so important to my children—not to mention my husband, who carries him around like a baby and coos to him—that my opinion has softened. He is really much less trouble than I would have imagined—less hassle, for example, than the four guinea pigs we went through before it registered that we just weren't cut out to be a rodent-owning family.

The thing about guinea pigs is that they don't really *do* anything. They're soft and cute and sort of cuddly to hold, but that's about it. You can achieve all those qualities with a stuffed animal and save yourself the trouble of a weekly cage cleaning. Guinea pigs also seem to be relatively delicate creatures, and when ours died one after another in the course of a few months (although never, conveniently enough, when my husband was home), I couldn't bear to keep replacing them.

The dog, on the other hand, has lasted for several years already, and I have been pleasantly surprised with the much-improved ratio of fun to nuisance in this pet. For one thing, Toby has a lively personality, as opposed to our guinea pigs, who had all the personality of a damp fur coat. He is filled with rapture at the arrival of any family member on the scene. He goes into quivering ecstasies at the mere mention of the word *walk*. He eats, with gusto, the same food every day of his life. Most of all, he loves to retrieve his ball.

Abandon any mental picture you may be harboring of a small, bouncy ball or a bright yellow tennis ball. Toby's ball is an ex-basketball, a large vinyl number that stays about three-quarters inflated and is almost as large as the dog himself. The game—and he never tires of it—is for you to kick or throw the ball across the yard, and he will go tearing after it, grab it in his teeth, and lug it back to you, shaking it around with a few ferocious growls before he drops it at your feet and starts barking maniacally for you to kick it again. I firmly believe that he would do this a thousand times in a row, if your foot would hold out that long, and every single time would be a fresh delight to him.

I have to confess that I feel a little old and stale by comparison. How different might my outlook be, I wonder, if I could summon the type of enthusiasm for the simple pleasures of my life that Toby does for his. The interesting thing is that, with a little extra attentiveness, I can.

Our daughter sent us a cassette tape she made on her mission in Zimbabwe, part of which she had recorded as she was washing her clothes in the bathtub in water she described as "questionable." She urged us on the tape to be thankful for everything we take for granted. So I determined to take one day to try to notice everything there was to be thankful for in the course of that day. Instead of grousing at my alarm clock, I thought how convenient it was to be automatically awakened when I needed to get up. It occurred to me immediately how lucky I was to be going across the hall rather than across the yard to get to the bathroom. A few minutes later, in the shower, I reveled in the comfortable sensations: the warm water pouring over me; the utterly clean smells of soap and shampoo; the silky feeling of my long hair sliding smoothly out of its tangles after I applied the conditioner to it. Shutting the water off, I wrapped myself in a fluffy, soft, American-Amazon-size towel that still smelled fresh from the dryer. And it went on from there.

Why are we not better able to recognize the huge blessings that lie all around us in our everyday world? I imagine it's largely because they're so common in the first place. We seem to have somehow become conditioned to the notion that the things really worth having are the ones only a few people have access to.

Witness the Cabbage Patch Kids phenomenon, for example. The year Cabbage Patch Kids hit the toy market, the demand far outstripped the supply, and rather than disappoint their children at Christmas, people went to extraordinary lengths to acquire those dolls. I personally know two families who bought them in Europe, somewhat to the amusement of vendors there, who couldn't understand why people who had come all the way to Rome would want a goofy-looking doll as a souvenir.

The next year at Christmas, when Cabbage Patch Kids were plentiful, most children weren't asking for them anymore. It was as if the veil had been removed from the consumers' eyes and people could suddenly see that the dolls were cute, but not *that* cute. When owning one was no longer a sign of status because anyone could get one, the only people who bought them were people who liked them for their own sake. The dolls continued to sell, but never with the fervor of that year of scarcity.

Because our Father in heaven has given us so many gifts in great abundance, we can easily fall into the trap of over-looking them entirely. I remember being enchanted as a tourist with the tiny daisies that grew everywhere in the grass at Hyde Park in England. My mother pointed out, "You know, people here probably think of them as weeds, the way we do with dandelions."

"Oh, but these are so much prettier . . ." I started to protest, and then I stopped and thought about dande-lions, bright little sunny things winking up from the grass, and I realized that those daisies probably weren't prettier at all, just novel to me. What a lovely gift, to have some kind of flower, whether it be dandelion or daisy, grow so profusely that little children always have something to gather for their mothers! From that day on, every time my children brought me a dandelion bouquet, I kept it for days in a small vase on the kitchen windowsill.

Dandelions, I have learned, can be as much a gift as a nuisance.

It's the same with lots of things in life. When you approach them with an attitude of adventure, many problems turn into challenges that can be almost like a game to overcome.

Think about video games for a minute. I can hardly even watch my children play them anymore, they have become so sophisticated. But I confess to a little addiction of my own to a computer game called "Lose Your Marbles." The premise is simple: each player has a rectangular field with two parallel lines crossing it horizontally right in the middle. The area between the lines is the width of one marble. Marbles of various colors appear, five across, in stacks in your rectangle, and you have to line them up with the computer's arrow keys so that marbles of the same color are next to each other in between the lines. When you get three or more in a row that way, they disappear. If you get four or five in a row, more marbles appear in your opponent's rectangle. The object of the game is to stay alive until your opponent's side is all filled up with marbles so that they can't be shifted around anymore.

If you can't understand the game from this hasty

explanation, don't worry. The only reason I bring it up at all is to point out that there are many things about the games we play that could operate to our benefit in our lives, if we would let them. For example, I now play "Lose Your Marbles" at the highest of the three skill levels offered, because otherwise it's too easy; it isn't any fun when I can win handily every time. This makes me think maybe I should stop whining about my life being too hard. Maybe I've chosen to play at this skill level!

In fact, with every child we added to the mix in our family, the skill level of my mothering game had to go up a notch. And, just as the difficulty increases in a video game with every obstacle you successfully overcome, the parenting challenges escalate as you safely navigate through the childhood years to arrive at the ultimate test of living with teenagers. If your children have lived long enough to hit puberty, you're already an expert player. Now the game changes altogether, and you get to play on a whole new field.

There is really no such thing as "winning" at "Lose Your Marbles." If you keep playing, it just keeps getting harder and harder until you are forced to bow to the superior skill of the computer. You can choose to stop playing, of course, but as long as you're in the game, it's going to increase in complexity. The joy is not in arriving but in traveling, getting a little better each time you play, advancing farther than you ever thought you could. If you fell into despair every time the computer won a game, you would never improve.

For a while I lived with the illusion that life would get easier as I got older, but it doesn't. The scenery changes, is all. If we make it successfully to the next level, we get a whole new set of problems to tackle, and we learn to be grateful for the tools we've picked up along the way that enable us to cope. And if we're smart, we recognize that there's no magical plateau that represents "winning," but that the joy is in progressing from level to level and advancing farther than we would have imagined possible.

The happiest people I know are the ones who seem to approach life from a problem-solving perspective rather than a problem-resenting one. I've seen many people succumb to bitterness over not having enough money, for example, and I contrast their attitude with that of a friend of mine who says, smiling, "I can take the green off a dollar." She can, too! Rather than whine about having less, she has achieved a very high skill level at doing more with less, to the extent that she and her husband have been able to travel to several exotic places in the world while I (with the same number of children and a higher gross income) gripe about scaring up enough gas money to get us to a hotel room a few miles away in Vernal.

The problems, it seems, are all part of the adventure. Imagine a video game with no enemies, no targets, no puzzles to solve, just a nice drive down a country street with trees and flowers lining the way. Boring! A story has to have conflict in order to be any good. Joy comes not from having a pain-free life but from conquering the obstacles even when they are painful.

I love the old Shaker hymn by James Russell Lowell, the first verse of which goes like this:

> *My life flows on in endless song.*
> *Above Earth's lamentation,*
> *I hear the real, though far-off, hymn*
> *That hails a new creation.*
> *Above the tumult and the strife*
> *I hear its music ringing.*
> *It sounds an echo in my soul—*
> *How can I keep from singing?*

There will always be tumult and strife, but there will also be music, and if I can hear the echo of it in my soul, I can always find cause for singing. Sometimes, though, it takes going through a period of noise and confusion to make the music audible.

The story of Lehi's family in the wilderness is a good example of this. We don't have much information in the account about Lehi's wife, Sariah, but I love to try to picture the events from her point of view. Knowing how I feel when my children come home late from a date, I can just imagine the agony she went through when her sons didn't return as quickly as expected with the brass plates from Jerusalem. It was a dangerous errand they were on, after all. What if they were lying dead on the roadside somewhere? Indeed, Nephi tells us that she got pretty upset with her husband: "Behold thou hast led us forth from the land of our inheritance, and my sons are no more, and we perish in the wilderness" (1 Nephi 5:2).

When the boys did return after having successfully completed their quest, her feelings changed substantially, "And she spake, saying: *Now* I know of a surety that the Lord hath commanded my husband to flee into the wilderness" (1 Nephi 5:8; emphasis added). Did she not know with that degree of surety until that trial had been overcome? Do you suppose that maybe that perilous part of the adventure was necessary in order to build Sariah's (and everyone's) faith? They would certainly need that increased faith as time went on and their circumstances became ever more challenging. What a blessing it was that one of their first experiences on their long journey offered such strong evidence of the Lord's guidance and protection!

"After much tribulation come the blessings," the Lord reminds us (D&C 58:4). I had an experience on a family vacation that helped me understand that principle better. We had taken our children to Bryce Canyon, and in the particular place where we had parked to look out from the scenic viewpoint, there was a well-marked trail that led down to the floor of the canyon, where hikers could actually be right in among all those amazing rock formations. It was early evening, but the marker at the trail head indicated that the walk was less than a mile, and we thought we could be well out of there before dark. So, anxious to experience the beauties of the canyon from close up, we headed down the path.

You may have deduced from earlier discussions that I am not much of a hiker. In fact, as an editor, I probably have the most sedentary job on the planet, and I don't do much to make up for that in my off hours, either. The walk down to the canyon floor was not too taxing, gravity being a good friend in such a situation. But it took quite a bit longer than I had anticipated to cross the flat part of the trail loop, and it was dusk by the time we got to the switchbacks that would return us to the rim of the canyon where we had started. After laboring up three or four of those little upward slices of trail, I knew I was in trouble. We seemed to be deep in a dark hole, and it was getting darker by the minute. The trail, fortunately, was clear and well defined, but there was no real way to mark our progress or see if we were really getting any closer to the top. I had to stop every five or six paces to catch my breath, and all my limbs were aching, but of course there was no choice but to press on.

Finally, I came around one of those sharp V-turns to find that the canyon wall behind me had ended and the most glorious full moon I had ever seen was rising, lighting the remainder of the path. The beautiful rock formations, no longer obscured from my view, were all edged in silver light, and the weariness dropped from me as I felt the hand of the Creator in the awe-inspiring view. I still had to push myself hard to get to the top of the trail, but it was no longer a tedious, frustrating process. Each time I had to stop and breathe heavily gave me another chance to enjoy the scenery.

I suppose if I had never ventured down the trail, I

would still have been impressed with that moonlit landscape as I saw it from the safe vantage point at the top. But I doubt whether it would have inspired in me the great love for the Lord and gratitude for his blessings that I felt as I was struggling up the mountainside. The blessing was there either way, but I received it differently because it had come "after much tribulation."

Life, it seems, is full of dark switchbacks, and sometimes the trail is long and winding and filled with sharp rocks. When I'm toiling along on an uphill stretch, I like to think that the moon might be waiting for me right around the corner. Sometimes I have to pause and catch my breath, and sometimes my progress seems mighty slow, but I have seen the hand of the Lord enough in my life that I trust him to keep me going. And when I get there—it's on to the next level of adventure!

Be Grateful for the Things You *Have* to Do

I clearly remember the first time I cooked dinner as a new bride after my husband and I returned from our honeymoon. We had a tiny apartment with an itty-bitty kitchen into which we had been able to squeeze a drop-leaf table that sat two. I could practically remain seated at the table and reach both the oven and the sink. Cooking in that kitchen was almost like playing with one of those child's plastic kitchen sets sold in toy stores.

I had lived away from home for several years, so cooking was not foreign to me. Maybe the cramped quarters were putting a crimp in my style on this particular evening. Or maybe I was just extra tired or hormonally challenged that day. Whatever the reason, I experienced a sensation quite new: It occurred to me in a blinding and none-too-happy flash that I was now going to have to fix dinner for the rest of my life. And not just fix it, but plan it—which was almost worse—and shop for it and clean up after it. It was almost more than I could bear to think about.

I'm not sure how long I was moody about that grim prospect. It was at least a few weeks. But eventually I noticed that I had stopped thinking about it, and started doing it, and one day flowed into another and they all trickled into the deeper rivers of the years passing by. Now those years are tranquil and swift-running, and the little pebbles in the bottom that represent such inescapables as cooking and doing laundry and attending parent-teacher conferences and paying for car repairs are scarcely enough to ripple the surface. They have become, instead of disturbances, the river bed that channels our family's life—the fundamental evidences of our greatest blessings.

Take the laundry, for example. Those never-ending piles represent an opulence of clothing almost unknown in a large percentage of the countries in the world. Imagine having so much excess clothing that multiple pieces can lie at the bottom of a basket for weeks and not really be missed! Imagine owning a machine into which you can toss the articles and have them come out fresh and sweet smelling!

Then there's cooking. The fact that I have to cook each day suggests that we live in a time and place where food is abundant. If I have to plan the meals, all that means is that we have a wide spectrum of possibilities to choose from. I get to exercise judgment and creativity on a daily basis in an activity that helps build unity, comfort, and physical strength in my family. I can stir up my special slow-cooked beef stew to calm us on a stormy day, or we can throw together a box of Hamburger Helper or something similarly quick and easy that leaves us time to dash off to other pursuits if the evening is booked. But because every member of my family needs to eat, I have the opportunity as the cook to make a meaningful connection with each of them every single day.

I realize that to some people this seems Pollyannaish to the point of gagging. "Terminally cheerful," as one of my friends puts it. But, hey, I just figure that if there's something I'm going to end up doing anyway, I might as well do my best to find some joy in it.

The truth is that our greatest blessings and our greatest trials seem to often come in the same package, and if we wish away the trials, we forgo the blessings as well. I saw a great episode of *The X-Files* on TV once in which the chief guest character was a genie who had to grant three wishes to anyone who unfurled her magic carpet. The trick was that she seemed to take a malicious delight in messing up those wishes by granting them in unforeseen and undesirable ways. For example, when the lead character tried to play it safe by wishing for "peace on earth," the genie killed off everybody in the world, and boy, was it peaceful! Waving away protests of "You know that's not what I meant," the genie pointed out, "You didn't specify."

I can think of a clear example in my own life of a trial I would happily have wished away on many occasions. One of our boys was a particularly lively toddler who thought nothing of dashing out into the street or spitting on other children's tricycle seats or throwing fistfuls of dirt at passersby. When I took him to my grandparents' home on Halloween dressed as an angel in a pillowcase and a tinsel halo, my grandfather hooted and said, "What's this— wishful thinking?" (This same grandfather once noticed something odd sticking out from under his microwave and found, upon investigation, thirty-seven Oreo tops where this kid and his siblings had stashed them after eating the cream out of the cookies.)

A particular challenge for us all was attending church,

where the long, open corridors seemed to beckon to our son as running lanes. We used to take him over to the ward building on weekdays to practice walking in the halls with his arms folded, but he rarely took more than a few steps before he was off at a high clip. I knew he wasn't being deliberately naughty, but his lively spirits could be exhausting, and I found myself frequently at my wit's end trying to keep up with him.

One day, I kept him home from preschool because he had a slight fever and didn't seem to feel too well. I was working in the kitchen while he napped on the hide-a-bed in the living room, when gradually I became aware of a strange, repeating, metallic sound, like a trampoline spring being stretched. When I finally went to investigate, I found my son in a full-blown seizure, unconscious and twitching. I called 911 and we dashed him up to Primary Children's Medical Center, where he was diagnosed with viral encephalitis and had to stay for several days. At any time during that vigil, as he lay so sick and listless in that bed, I would have given almost any amount of money to be chasing that boy down the hall at church.

Fortunately, he recovered completely, and I never resented his lively spirits again as I had before. It was all part of the package that was my son, and I was so grateful that I had it to put up with.

I can see now that everything I *have* to do represents a connection with the world, an intersection with life where I can make a contribution. I well remember the period of life when I was a young adult living away from home but in the same city as my parents, and it occurred to me one day that if I dropped right off the face of the earth, no one would even know for at least a week. My roommates would assume I had gone home for a while, and my parents would assume I was living my usual life in my apartment. My teachers wouldn't notice—they don't slap you with big citizenship penalties if you don't show up for a class in college. I didn't *have* to be anywhere, and that generated in me the most peculiar identity crisis, a sense of "non-ness" that was almost numbing.

As frustrating as it can be to have so many people needing me these days, at least I know I would be missed almost immediately if I disappeared. That's sort of comforting. Everything I have to do means I have used my agency to reach out and commit to something or someone. Granted, this can be agonizing, as the act of choosing almost always requires the simultaneous *unchoosing* of many alternatives. But if there are things you *have* to do, you can embrace them with your full heart and not waste time looking back or battling with divided loyalties.

Motherhood is the kind of whole-souled commitment that requires a woman to leave many things behind, at least temporarily. I think there's a reason—beyond the obvious physiological one—why the program begins with middle-of-the-night feedings. Don't get me wrong: I cheered when my children began sleeping through the night. But once you're actually *up* in the wee hours of the morning, and it's just you and the little one and the utter stillness, it can be kind of magical. That baby may not be able to talk, but there is a level of spirit-to-spirit communication that's easier to tune in to when the rest of the world is quiet.

You need to store up those tender feelings, because they have a tendency to fade as the child approaches the age of two. I have seen several times on the Internet, attributed to various sources, this quotation: "Living with small children is like being pecked to death by ducklings." This is a solemn truth. It's just that their needs are so constant, and they're so persistent in demanding that you meet them. Couple that with the fact that they're just big enough to actually do serious injury to themselves and each other, so they have to be watched *all the time,* and you'll know why so many mothers of toddlers walk around with that glazed look on their faces.

People who have never had little children don't get this. If you've ever dealt with a two-year-old in full-blown tantrum state in a grocery store, you probably understand how lepers felt in biblical times. It's impossible to explain to everyone you wheel past that you had to take a stand before the child imbibed an entire bottle of ranch dressing. They don't comprehend that two-year-olds want what they want, when they want it, and are not generally amenable to even the most reasonable of suggestions. To the childless, you're just a rotten parent, and your kid is a brat, and you shouldn't be allowed out in public together. But if you're going to have children, they're going to be two years old at some point, and you just have to learn to deal with it.

It helps (a little) to remember that most "have-to's" start out as choices. I'm certain I have looked every one of my children in the eyes at least once and said, "We *asked* Heavenly Father to send you to us!" I know I have repeated that sentiment over and over in my mind, almost as a mantra, as I have hauled screaming babies out of sacrament meetings, listened to wailing toddlers kick their bedroom doors as they worked off their tantrums, foraged frantically through backpacks for missing permissions notes and overdue homework, and lain in bed at night listening for the teenagers' car to pull into the driveway. These little bumps on the parenting highway are not the product of some mischievous genie saying, "You didn't specify." They're part of an agreement we made to allow one of Heavenly Father's precious children, who has just as much agency as we do, to be born into our home and into the eternal sealing covenant we made when we got married.

Some people see such commitment as a restriction. I prefer to think of it as a form, like a sonnet is a form for poetry. When you write a poem, you can do it any way you like, of course, but if you choose to make it a sonnet you have automatically imposed upon yourself a certain rhyme scheme and rhythmic pattern. Step outside the form, and you will not have a sonnet.

Given that restriction, why would anyone choose to write a sonnet in preference to, say, a poem in free verse? The beauty of it is that when you are working within the set parameters of the sonnet form, you have to choose your words more carefully. You have to be more economic and selective with your syllables. Every word settles into a certain, inevitable spot, and when that spot is right, the poem is almost alive. The joy of writing a sonnet that really works is well worth the effort it takes to do it.

When you choose mothering, you've chosen a form for your life. You have instantly imposed upon yourself a certain level of responsibility. You will have to choose more carefully where to put your resources, particularly your time and energy and probably your money as well. But as those elements settle into spots that seem right, your family comes to life and there is joy in it.

Of course, when you're in the middle of it, it doesn't feel like you're choosing anything at all. The money flies out into the hands of grocery store clerks, gas station attendants, and those nice folks at VISA, usually before it has even had a chance to light in your bank account. Time disappears like water being sucked into parched earth; you start out every day with what seems like an ample pitcherful, and by the time you've filled all the glasses people are holding out, there's barely a trickle left for you. As for energy, all I can say is I'm just so grateful Heavenly Father gives us a night for every day, because usually by the time bedtime rolls around, I feel like a guttering candle. When our children were little, I was physically exhausted a good deal of the time. Now that they're older, the demands are more emotionally and mentally fatiguing. Some nights, after a particularly trying bout with homework assignments, I drop into bed with my whole brain hurting.

One useful trick is to spend some time figuring out what you want to do, and then look for ways to make the have-to's play into it. For example, once our teenagers hit driving age, we seem to see less and less of them (which is a pity, because they're actually pretty good company by then). I always wish we had time to talk, even just to touch base once in a while and be sure everything is running smoothly.

We have a little junker car that our high-school-age son drives to school, but his father had to commandeer it one fall when we went through a bout of auto-repair problems (those always come in flocks, don't they?) and were short one vehicle for an extended period. So I had to drag myself out and drive that kid to school for several weeks.

I grumbled about this at first. Doing the school drop seemed to eat up my whole morning, even though I knew it would only take fifteen minutes for the round trip. To begin with, I had to throw some clothes on so that if I got in an accident in the high-school parking lot I wouldn't embarrass my son. (I'm beyond being embarrassed myself at being seen in my robe before 8:00 in the morning.) Since we have only one bathroom, and mine is the latest work schedule, I don't get a shower slot that early in the morning, so this meant I had to get dressed twice every morning. Then, after making the high-school drop, I would pull into the driveway barely in time to run into the house and holler at the junior-high kid, who seems to exist in a parallel universe where time flows more slowly, "Aren't you ready *yet?*" A mad dash to the junior high would leave me just enough time to shower and dress for work before child number three had to be deposited at the elementary school. It seemed just cause for murmuring, and murmur I did, although in my case it took more the form of muttering and stomping around.

About a week into this, I realized that I had a golden, seven-minute nugget of time every single morning when that high-school boy was all mine. I began to think up questions to ask him and stories to tell him in those moments when he was a captive audience. We had some really great seven-minute conversations, and I learned more about what was going on in his life than I had been privy to for most of the year. I was actually a little sad when our car woes were finally resolved and he could drive himself again.

Another example: I want to be able to share more time with our youngest child, but there never seem to be enough hours in the day. When I do actually fix dinner, which happens at least a few times a week, I like to have her help me. She enjoys cooking, I appreciate the company, and it's a block of time I have to devote to the task anyway, so it doesn't feel like it gets subtracted from the "time budget" for the day.

Finally, sometimes you just have to turn a *want-to* into a *have-to* in order to make it happen. I joined a local chorus when I still had small children in order to have an assured night when I simply had to leave the house—it was a commitment. What a glorious feeling to *have* to be in a place where no one (including me) could expect me to do anything except something I loved to do in the first place! I couldn't answer a phone or throw in a load of laundry or drag myself through an algebra problem. I couldn't scour the toilet or fumigate the boys' room or even sit in front of the TV set feeling guilty for not doing any of the items on my endless list of chores. All I could do was sing my heart out, and I got to do it in a room full of other adults who could actually read music and sing mostly on key. (I broke into tears my first night there just during the warm-ups, I was so moved by the strength of the men's section.) If you can get just one want-to onto your have-to list in this way, it changes the feeling of the whole list.

Remember, everything you have to do means you belong to someone and something. One of the greatest surprises, and greatest joys, comes as you realize that those have-to's in your life actually got you where you wanted to be all along!

Remember That the Years Fly By, Even though Some of the Days Are Mighty Long

In our days of parenting small children, we used to go quite often on evening walks around the block. I would push the baby in the stroller, and the three-year-old always insisted on bringing her "bike," a cumbersome plastic affair that was too low to the ground for a parent to comfortably push and too unwieldy to carry easily. It seemed like her little legs always wore out before we got home, and we generally spent the last stretch coaxing her along, pushing her a few feet at a time to keep her going, and ultimately carrying the baby *and* the bike so the toddler could ride in the stroller.

On one of those evenings I was not in a patient mood when we started out, and I tried to put my foot down about the bike. I thought it would be easier if all we had to carry was the child. But she wasn't going anywhere without her bike, and as the conflict escalated, I succumbed, the walk being more important to me at that moment than winning the power struggle. I did, however, extract a solemn promise from that child that she would be responsible to get both herself and her bike home.

Sure enough, about a block and a half from the house, she just couldn't push those pedals anymore. I was in the middle of my "What did I tell you?" speech, and we were arguing about keeping promises and what needed to happen next, when the neighbors in front of whose house we had stopped drove into their driveway. "Oh, your children are getting so big!" exclaimed the woman as she got out of the car. "Don't you just adore them at this age? It goes by way too fast!"

Well, at that point, it couldn't have gone by too fast for me, but I smiled and tried to be polite. My friend obviously saw through me, because she said, "I know you don't believe this right now, but the years will fly by before you realize it, and you will barely remember what this phase of life feels like."

I didn't want to admit that she might be right, partly because it seemed to minimize the struggle I was going through, but eighteen years later, I'm here to tell you that what my friend said is true. Each phase of child rearing seems unending when you're in the middle of it, but once it has passed, and you're on to the next challenge, the last one seems almost like a dream.

My daughter and I attended BYU Women's Conference together one year, and we arrived a little late for the opening session and ended up sitting on the bleacher-style seats in the Marriott Center, opposite the speaker's platform. During the course of that session, we noticed about half a row of empty seats up toward the top of the arena on the other side, and we took note of the section number and agreed that we would climb up there for the next class.

The speech ended, and we ran out and around the concourse to the proper section, but as we started to climb the stairs, our view of the top was blocked and we could no longer see the seats up there. Confident that we had noted the place correctly, though, we continued to scale the heights, my daughter exercising great patience as I began to huff and puff, and, sure enough, when we got to the top those seats were available. If we hadn't seen them from our far-off perspective, we would not have known they were there, and if we hadn't felt sure they were there, we would never have made the climb.

As mothers, we don't often get the benefit of that far-off perspective that assures us we're moving in the right direction. But, with faith and prayer and patience, we somehow manage to make our way through each of the stages of our children's lives. And the perspective of others who have made the climb before us can be of at least some help. With that in mind, I'd like to share a little of what I've found along the motherhood trail, dividing the experiences into the things you just have to live through and the things you're going to want to be careful not to forget. Of course, I've had to impose some arbitrary age boundaries on the categories; it's not as tidy as all that in real life. And not everything will apply to everybody. But these are some general observations that seem to hold true with a lot of moms I know.

PHASE 1: PREGNANCY AND CHILDBIRTH

It took us a couple of years to get pregnant with our first child, so we were ecstatic when it actually happened. I was fortunate enough to have a relatively uncomplicated time. I was tired but not especially sick, as contrasted with my coworker who was also pregnant and who threw up every day in the elevator on the way to work. If you've ever been to Relief Society, you know that women adore sharing their experiences with pregnancy, labor, and delivery, so the following ideas are a fair amalgam of many women's experiences.

You just have to live through:

1. Days and weeks and sometimes months on end of never feeling quite in control of yourself. You will cry over television commercials, especially the really touching ones showing people calling their mothers long distance or feeding oatmeal to their grandchildren. You will know the location of the rest rooms in every store and public place you enter for the next nine months. You will learn to make sure there's a clear path from your side of the bed to the bathroom that can be safely navigated in the middle of the night.

2. Wearing the same clothes until you are so sick of them you will want to burn them at the end of the pregnancy. Unless you have a lot more money than most of the women I know, you're probably going to be stuck with a fairly limited wardrobe, especially when it comes to nice dresses. It helps if you have sisters or friends who are willing to share!

3. People's stunningly insensitive remarks: "Whoa, you're not due for another six weeks? You look like you're ready to pop!" "Are you sure it isn't twins? You look awfully big to be carrying just one baby," or, my favorite,

"Isn't that baby here *yet?*" "Oh, yeah, she's here," I always wanted to say, "I'm just keeping her under my dress so she doesn't get your germs on her." Just remember, it could be worse: someone could say "Isn't your baby here yet?" after you've already *had* the baby. That's happened to me too.

4. Labor and delivery. No gory stories, I promise. Just remember, it doesn't last forever and it's worth it.

You're going to want to remember:

1. What it felt like the moment you learned you were going to have a baby.

2. The first time you felt the baby move and knew for real that this was actually a live person growing inside you. You'll feel similar feelings when you hear the baby's heartbeat and see it on a sonogram. Ultrasound imaging was relatively new when we were having our babies, and our last child was the only one who we actually saw before she was born. They gave us a video, which is pretty boring now because we don't have the nurse there to point out the various body parts, but it was miraculous when we were seeing it "live."

3. Labor and delivery—not the pain, but the intense feelings of being on the brink of eternity as new life comes into the world.

PHASE 2: INFANTS

The joy and the trial of having a tiny baby is that this is a real live person who is totally dependent on you for everything. It's a wonderful and sacred feeling to be so needed—and it's also an exhausting one. No amount of reading or planning or preparation can impress upon you what it truly means to add a new little person to your family. You get to find this out for yourself!

You just have to live through:

1. Ongoing sleep deprivation. This can make you a little crazy after a few weeks. Remind yourself when you feel out of control that this is a natural physiological reaction to having to get up in the middle of the night on a regular basis. You'll survive it.

2. Being on call 24/7. This is especially true if you're nursing, which I recommend even though it's harder than it looks, because it's healthier for the baby and a whole lot cheaper and more convenient than formula. Even if you're using a bottle, though, you're the mom, and if there's a problem any hour of the day or night, you're the go-to woman.

3. Cleaning up messes. For such a little person, a baby can go through a whale of a lot of diapers and burp cloths

and outfits in a day. Just plan on spending more time in the laundry room.

4. A certain amount of unexplained irritability in your child. Sometimes babies cry for no discernible reason, and they continue to cry after you've fed them and diapered them and rocked them and done everything you can think of. Don't panic—and don't be embarrassed. It's helpful to have something to blame it on if such an outburst should occur in public—teething is the most common scapegoat.

You're going to want to remember:

1. The astounding feeling of watching an infant figure out the world. There will be a day when she is captivated by her hands, for example, and a time when he notices his feet. This is why everything goes in the mouth when the child gets mobile enough—just another way of gathering information.

2. Firsts, especially the baby's first word. All my children want to know what their first word was, and I didn't write it down so I can't remember for any of them. It would have been so easy to do! (Guilt, guilt, shame, and assorted horrible-mother sentiments.)

3. What it feels like to be somebody's favorite person in the whole wide world.

PHASE 3: TODDLERS AND PRESCHOOLERS

If you're getting a full night's sleep now, it's a lucky thing, because you're going to need all your energy to keep up with a child who can walk and run and open doors unassisted. So much growing occurs during these years, and moms have to be constantly alert for both the danger and the excitement.

You just have to live through:

1. Tantrums. These are not a signal of your ineptness as a mother, although you will feel as if they are. They're usually just a manifestation of the frustration that children feel when their desires exceed their capacities. Unless you're in a position to give your children everything they want at the exact moment they want it for the rest of their lives (heaven forbid!), you're going to have to put up with some tantrums.

2. Toilet training. Just take a deep breath and do it. Don't worry that you have to bribe them at first—do you know a single fifth-grader who has to be paid M&Ms to use the bathroom?

3. An obsessive need to have things done in a particular way time after time. If you don't put the hair bow in the exact right spot, be prepared for tears. A corollary to

this one is the child who *must* do everything himself or herself. You'll save yourself some grief if you allow extra time for getting dressed in the morning and if you learn not to be too particular about coordinating clothing colors.

4. Clinginess. This varies from child to child, of course, but the uncertainty of the big, bad world seems to send everyone running back to Mom at some point. This is especially true if you have another baby while child number one is in the toddler stage. Even the most independent children need reassurance that their world is going to stay together when a new baby enters it.

You're going to want to remember:

1. The funny things your kids say and do. I *was* astute enough to jot down a few choice happenings and statements from each of my children as they were growing up, and one of their favorite games now is "Tell me about the cute things I did when I was little." I know their own children are going to love knowing these things too.

2. How completely adorable they can be. If you can't afford a video camera, borrow or rent one a couple of times a year, not just on birthdays or Christmas but to capture a regular day of life. Even if you have only a few such recordings, they are great treasures.

3. The fascination of a budding personality that grows by leaps and bounds as new experiences are added.

4. The unquenchable enthusiasm for life that allows a small child to enjoy the same activities over and over again.

PHASE 4: AGES 5 THROUGH 11

The world of elementary school beckons, and not a moment too soon! These are the years of running around, of PTA and soccer and instrument rentals and activities designed to help your children find their special skills. They're also a welcome breather between tumultuous toddlerhood and fiery adolescence.

You just have to live through:

1. Long division and word searches. These are the symbols of the hours you will spend dragging an elementary-school-age child through homework after the poor kid has already spent nearly seven hours in school. Teachers who think they are assigning only fifteen minutes' worth of math homework in an evening have clearly never plopped a child down at the table with a page of long-division problems. I've tried offering treats for finished problems, setting the timer to have a race against the clock, pointing and talking the kid through the steps, and

just about anything else you might think of. And I have yet to find a teacher who can explain to me the educational value of a word search, so when my kids bring those huge, daunting squares full of scrambled letters home, I really cringe. We usually do the word searches together as a family; otherwise it would take the child a couple of hours at least.

2. Being a taxi service. You've got to get the kid to and from school in the first place, which may or may not entail driving but probably will at least part of the time. Then there are assorted extracurricular activities, and friends' houses might be out of walking or even biking range. Add Primary or Cub Scouting activities and running to the store for glue sticks and poster board.

3. School fund-raisers. It seems like every time you turn around, your child is bringing home a colorful brochure hawking chocolates or wrapping paper or magazine subscriptions, and it always comes with an auxiliary brochure featuring a dazzling array of prizes available to be won by the enterprising young salesperson. I've gotten to the point where I send five bucks to the school in an envelope and then just buy the kid the pencil topper or the googly goggles or the mini-flashlight he might have won. It's cheaper that way.

You're going to want to remember:

1. The excitement of helping a child learn to read. Gaining access to the world of books is an incomparable adventure that you will love sharing with your children. You can almost feel their brains expanding as they work out the concepts of phonetics and blending and discover the way those little black marks on white paper actually stand for words and stories.

2. How your child looked the day he or she was baptized.

3. The fascinating questions children ask as they experience more of the world. They offer some fairly amazing observations as well. Once when we were all in the car together our little girl complained that she was cold. Her seven-year-old brother piped up, "If you were a lizard, you wouldn't be cold. Your body would be the same temperature as the air around it." That is Phase 4 wisdom at its finest!

PHASE 5: AGES 12 THROUGH 15

Take a deep breath! This little phase is like transition labor: a lot of heavy pain because things are really starting to happen now. As with toddlers, an adolescent's desires often exceed capacities, and that little formula for frustration will play into a lot of your interactions with young teenagers.

You just have to live through:

1. The child's tendency to consider himself or herself the center of all meaningful activity and emotion in the world. Children of this age filter everything through a dense screen of "How does this affect *me?*" They don't have much regard for how it might affect anyone else. A typical exchange:

Daughter: "Mom, could you please drop us off at the movie? It starts in ten minutes."

Mom (leaping to feet and grabbing keys): "Sure, honey."

Daughter: "Are you going to come dressed like *that?*"

2. Quantum leaping from exhilaration to despair, with little in between. And the scale usually tips to the despair side. This is hormonal, so don't even try to apply logic to it. Just prepare to do a lot of nodding and smiling and looking sympathetic.

3. Junior high. In some areas it's middle school, but the agony is the same. It is the most wretched stretch of the whole school experience, mostly because kids are unilaterally insecure at this age, and they take it out on each other. Another factor is that there is such a disparity in

physical growth in junior high kids. Face it, your child is going to get stomped on, emotionally at least if not physically as well. Home needs to be the healing place, so curb the urge to lash back when the humiliation they've endured manifests itself in immature behavior.

You're going to want to remember:

1. That almost magical transition between Primary and Mutual. Your girl is a young woman now. Your boy is a holder of God's holy priesthood. Believe me, they feel it!

2. The little breakthroughs that signal a growing awareness of the gospel. Their testimony is being fed from lots of different sources at this point. And since you as a parent have probably lost credibility for a season just by virtue of *being* the parent, the influence of Sunday School teachers and Mutual and quorum leaders and seminary instructors takes on greater importance. It is wonderful to see your child embracing a gospel concept that didn't come from you!

3. Lots of firsts: first baby-sitting job, first time passing the sacrament, first stake dance, first youth conference, first day of non-elementary school. You'll think of more.

PHASE 6: AGES 16 AND UP

Finally, finally, they turn civil again! A lot of good that does, though, because you'll be lucky to catch a glimpse of them at home now and then. New mobility, new attachments to outside interests and friends, and a new sense of independence will draw them away more and more as the years go by. The good thing is, they come back as friends.

You just have to live through:

1. Fender benders. Every teenager has them, or at least insurance companies charge as if this were so. We're three for three in our own family so far. Make sure they buckle up, and try to put them in a car you don't care too much about.

2. Increased expenses. Anyone who thinks a high school education in America is free doesn't have kids that old yet. The typical school year starts out with a hefty registration fee, and then many classes tack on an additional ten to twenty dollars for labs or supplies or field trips. Add the cost of yearbooks, uniforms for sports teams or musical groups, gym clothes, and school supplies (don't forget the $100 calculator), and the sticker shock of putting a kid through high school is just that—a shock.

Personal costs can soar as well. What we have shelled out over the years for face wash and deodorant and hair-care products alone would probably equal the gross national product of a small third-world country.

3. Saying good-bye. There will be a lot of little

mini-partings, all of them preludes to the grand parting that means they're off into the world to start families of their own.

You're going to want to remember:

1. The fun of meeting their friends and watching them get involved in dating and school activities and just general sociability.

2. The times when they landed long enough to have really great talks with you. Sometimes they even want to hear what *you* have to say, which is a welcome change from the last phase!

3. The joy of every Big Event, and those are coming fast and furious now. Getting the driver's license. Going on that first date. Making the team, or the cast, or the club, or the musical group. Getting the mission call. Finding "the one." Every step fills your heart—but it will tug at the strings, too, because each is a step away from you.

PHASE 7: GRANDPARENTING

I'm not there yet, but everyone claims it's the most fun of all. I'm just glad there's more to look forward to!

I make a lot of mistakes as a mother, but I've decided the biggest mistake of all would be to dwell on the frustrations of the "live-throughs" while letting the "want-to-remembers" slip through my fingers. There is so much joy in every phase of a child's life that it seems a shame to make it hostage to the problems that inevitably crop up. The days may seem long, but the years will get away from you if you're not careful. Overlook what you can, correct what you have to, pour love into every decision you make, and you'll look back without regret.

EPILOGUE

It's Worth It

As a woman in the twenty-first century, you're going to hear from a lot of different sources that Being the Mom isn't worth it. They'll tell you it's tedious, and that can certainly be true. (However, couldn't that be said of any job, at least sometimes?) They'll warn you about being unnoticed and underappreciated, and you'll acknowledge that much of what you do seems invisible (unless you leave it undone for a day or two). They'll tell you you're wasting your talent and not accomplishing anything, but that's because they're not patient enough to watch until the fruits of your labors reach maturity.

What these detractors of motherhood don't seem to get is that the story of the world is not about *them*. It's not about any individual, no matter how much fame or money or power or respect that person acquires. It's all about learning—learning who we are and how to love each other and what we need to do to get back to our Father in heaven. And the school of motherhood seems to offer exactly those courses.

Being the Mom teaches you who you are because you have to reach into the deepest parts of yourself to summon the mental and emotional resources to do the job. You will find yourself accomplishing things you would never have dreamed you were capable of, simply because they have to be done.

Being the Mom gives you opportunities to exercise love in all its dimensions: patient love, exuberant love, adoring love, tough love, affectionate love, enduring love, and always, always unconditional love. If, as John says, "God is love" (1 John 4:8), doesn't it make sense that you would draw closer to God the more you practice this divine attribute? As the Mom, you'll get plenty of practice!

Finally, being the Mom reveals to you every day what you need to do to return to your Father in heaven. After all, *mother* is one of the few titles you'll take with you when you go. The family you are helping build represents the only unit on earth that is designed to last through eternity. It's not a waste of your talent—it's the most significant possible use of it!

I can't imagine that any woman loves what she's doing every hour of every day, and when things get tough, it's easy to second-guess yourself. The fact that such a wonderful array of choices is available to women today makes it easy to think (especially in those less-rewarding moments) that maybe you chose wrong.

You didn't.

No one can properly assess the value of what you do because they're not there to see all the little ways in which you are "paid" and how the world is blessed by your efforts.

Someday, closer to the end of your life, when your grandchildren and great-grandchildren are running around in the yard and climbing up to give you sticky kisses and writing you love notes, I'll bet it will be clearer—to everyone—who made the right choice. And in eternity, when you're sitting surrounded by your posterity and enjoying the sweet companionship of a multitude of loved ones, those people who tried to tell you otherwise in this life will understand what you knew all along: Being the Mom is the best!

About the Author

Emily Watts is a lover of words. She has been an editor for Deseret Book Company for more than twenty years, much of that time working from home part-time so she could devote full attention to her five children: Natalie, Brandon, Trevor, Dylan, and Sylvia. She also sings in the Utah Symphony Chorus and makes really great chocolate chip cookies. The co-presenter (with John Bytheway) of the talk tape *Women Are, That They Might Have Joy Too*, she has also published poetry and short stories. *Being the Mom* is her first full-length book. She and her husband, Larry, live in Salt Lake City.